The Power of Guidance

Teaching Social-Emotional
Skills in Early Childhood Classrooms

Join us on the web at
www.cengage.com/education

The Power of Guidance
Teaching Social-Emotional Skills in Early Childhood Classrooms

Dan Gartrell

DELMAR
CENGAGE Learning

Australia • Brazil • Japan • Korea • Mexico • Singapore • Spain • United Kingdom • United States

DELMAR
CENGAGE Learning™

The Power of Guidance:
Teaching Social-Emotional
Skills in Early Childhood
Classrooms
Dan Gartrell

Career Education SBU:
Vice President, Dawn Gerrain

Director of Editorial:
Sherry Gomoll

Acquisitions Editor:
Erin O'Connor

Editorial Assistant: Ivy Ip

Director of Production:
Wendy A. Troeger

Production Manager:
Carolyn Miller

Production Editor: Joy Kocsis

Director of Marketing:
Donna J. Lewis

Channel Manager: Nigar Hale

Cover Design:
Joseph Villanova

Composition: Carlisle
Communications, Inc.

National Association for the
Education of Young Children
1509 16th Street, NW
Washington, DC 20036-1426
800-424-2460
www.naeyc.org

For product information and technology assistance,
contact us at
**Cengage Learning Customer & Sales Support,
1-800-354-9706**

For permission to use material from this text or product,
submit all requests online at
www.cengage.com/permissions
Further permissions questions can be emailed to
permissionrequest@cengage.com

Library of Congress Control Number: 2003013311
ISBN-13: 978-1-4018-4856-9
ISBN-10: 1-4018-4856-7

Delmar
10 Davis Drive
Belmont, CA 94002-3098
USA

Cengage Learning is a leading provider of customized learning solutions with office locations around the globe, including Singapore, the United Kingdom, Australia, Mexico, Brazil, and Japan. Locate your local office at: **www.cengage.com/global**

Cengage Learning products are represented in Canada by Nelson Education, Ltd.

To learn more about Delmar, visit **www.cengage.com/delmar**

Purchase any of our products at your local college store or at our preferred online store **www.ichapters.com**

NOTICE TO THE READER

Publisher does not warrant or guarantee any of the products described herein or perform any independent analysis in connection with any of the product information contained herein. Publisher does not assume, and expressly disclaims, any obligation to obtain and include information other than that provided to it by the manufacturer.

The reader is expressly warned to consider and adopt all safety precautions that might be indicated by the activities herein and to avoid all potential hazards. By following the instructions contained herein, the reader willingly assumes all risks in connection with such instructions.

The publisher makes no representation or warranties of any kind, including but not limited to, the warranties of fitness for particular purpose or merchantability, nor are any such representations implied with respect to the material set forth herein, and the publisher takes no responsibility with respect to such material. The publisher shall not be liable for any special, consequential, or exemplary damages resulting, in whole or part, from the readers' use of, or reliance upon, this material.

Printed in Canada
7 8 9 10 11 10 09

For my Mother,
Beth Twiggar Goff,
who raised us this way
and whose last story,
published at age 87,
provides a beacon for all those who
really like to write

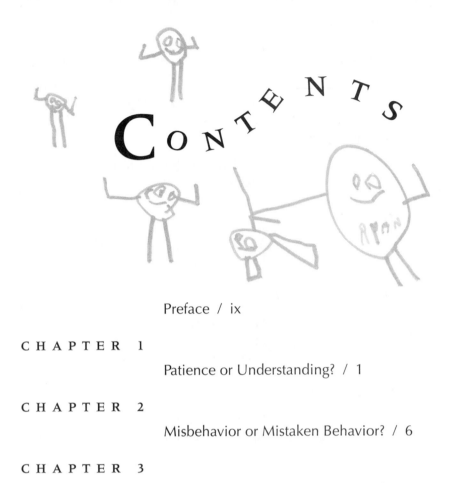

Contents

PREFACE

Dear Reader,

I am honored to bring you this book exploring "the power of guidance." The 11 chapters (including two by colleagues) were written over 15 years' time. Nine chapters originally appeared as articles in *Young Children,* which is published by the National Association for the Education of Young Children (NAEYC), or as material in my two books: *A Guidance Approach for the Encouraging Classroom,* (3rd ed.) (Delmar Learning, 2003) and *What the Kids Said Today: Using Classroom Conversations to Become a Better Teacher* (Redleaf Press, 2000). Two chapters are new, written for this book. The chapters follow a chronological sequence, an order that hopefully shows progress in our thinking about guidance over the years.

The chapters are all different. One, the introductory chapter is just a few pages, and another is as long as that textbook chapter you don't want to meet in your dreams. Some chapters fit together as though written as a set (two were). The sequence of others—in particular Chapter 4 on Family-Teacher Partnerships—may seem at first glance to be out of place. To ease the transition from one chapter to the next, all begin with "quick takes," which are author notes that bridge the gap and set the scene. Because most chapters were done first for other publications, there may be an occasional hint of familiarity in content from one chapter to another. Since multiple exposures to newer ideas is often advantageous, I hope you will regard this happening more as "reinforcement of important concepts from differing contexts," than as simply repetition.

CONSIDERATIONS

■ The **age range** addressed in the book needs a few words. A former Head Start and elementary school teacher, my professional expertise as a teacher and teacher-educator has centered on "older young children," aged three (or when toddlers in child care first join that preschool group) to aged eight. If you visualize a typical 33-month-old and a typical just-nine-year-old, the period of six years plus is a tremendous period of time. So much physical development, brain development, and personality development occur during this span that the three-to eight-year-old range seems plenty for what these chapters address.

■ Besides many cited references in each chapter, and hopefully cogent discussion, I illustrate points frequently with anecdotes from early childhood classrooms. When used to illustrate rather than "prove" a point, the practical teaching value of anecdotes can be high. One challenge in presenting complex ideas through anecdotes, however, is that they tend to "peg" a practice to the age group portrayed. For instance, a reader who teaches four-year-olds may be at a loss for what to take from an anecdote about a class meeting in a primary-grade classroom.

My strategy was to provide anecdotes in each chapter that represent a variety of age levels throughout the developmental span. Whether or not this accommodation works, my intent is *not* to suggest that the specifics of any practice can be applied in a literal manner to children who are developmentally younger or older. Developmentally appropriate practice—a common denominator for every chapter in the book—means that teachers *adapt* ideas to the unique circumstances of the children in their classes—and do not rigidly "adopt and impose" ideas. Guidance, as the essence of developmentally appropriate practice, requires enlightened professional judgment on the part of the adults in charge.

■ In line with the anecdotes, some readers may find my writing style informal in tone. My goal as a writer has always been to make important ideas about teaching young children accessible and worth thinking about, but not watered down. Toward this end, these chapters emulate the spirit and language of the noted 20th Century psychologist, Haim Ginott: "To reach a child's mind, a teacher must capture his heart." (Ginott—hard sounds on the consonants.) Consistently in his writing—and especially in his 1972 classic, *Teacher and Child*, (New York: Avon), Ginott used language that balanced researched ideas with readable pages.

The author and Delmar Learning make every effort to ensure that all Internet resources are accurate at the time of printing. However, due to the fluid, time-sensitive nature of the Internet, we cannot guarantee that all URLs and Web site addresses will remain current for the duration of this edition.

ACKNOWLEDGMENTS

Two fellow writers have made significant contributions to the *The Power of Guidance*. Nancy Weber of Bay City, Michigan, wrote the first chapter "Patience or Understanding?"; word-for-word the book's most potent item. Written in 1987 for *Young Children,* her mini-intro chapter stands the test of time and sets the stage for the rest of the book.

Margaret King, of Ohio University–Athens, crafted the contents of Chapter Eight, "Guidance with Boys in Early Childhood Classrooms." The chapter was excerpted in a recent issue of *Young Children,* but is published in its entirety for the first time here. I worked with her on the chapter, but Margaret is first author.

As further content acknowledgment, Chapter 11 gives an account of how to use the *Position Booklet* of the Minnesota Association for the Education of Young Children, *Developmentally Appropriate Guidance of Young Children,* as a training tool. The Booklet can be used with staff, parents, and outside professionals. For information about the booklet, contact Deborah Fitzwater-Dewey, Executive Director of MnAEYC, at *dfitzwater-dewey@aeyc.mn-org*

Earlier, I mentioned that anecdotes appear frequently in the book to illustrate guidance points. Many former students have contributed anecdotes for my writing, submitted when they were practicum students, student teachers, or teachers. I have acknowledged many of these contributors in another book of mine, based entirely on anecdotes, but would like to especially thank four here who have each contributed more than one: Julie Curb, Pat Sanford, Sharon Hoverson, and Marta Underthun. The contributed stories enliven these pages.

The author would also like to thank the following reviewers, enlisted by Delmar Learning, for their helpful suggestions and constructive criticism:

Alice Beyrent
Hesser College
Manchester, NH

Victoria Folds, EdD
Tutor Time Learning Systems
Boca Raton, FL

Mary Lou Brotherson, EdD
Barry University
Miami, FL

Robin Hasslen, PhD
St. Cloud State University
St. Cloud, MN

Mary Cordell
Navarro College
Corsicana, TX

I would also like to express gratitude to Delmar Learning of Clifton Park, New York, and Redleaf Press of St. Paul for permission to adapt and reproduce material from my books with these two publishers.

Production thanks go first to Carol Copple, Publications Director of the National Association for the Education of Young Children, for supporting this project and helping to bring it to completion. Gratitude is also expressed to Erin O'Connor and Joy Kocsis along with all of the competent Delmar Learning staff, and to Triple SSS Press Media Development and Carlisle Communications for seeing the project through. Only because of the sustained efforts of these solid professionals, the book has come together as it has.

OTHER THOUGHTS

My writing over the years has happened in Bemidji and St. Paul, Minnesota, in West Nyack, New York, and in Berlin, Germany. My wife, my mother, our children, and grandchildren are no doubt glad that I have promised a break from writing across the next string of visits. Mostly, though, the writing happened in Bemidji, and you could say that the book is a product of the Midwest—though the ideas behind it have been well received on both coasts and, in fact, in other countries. (And Haim Ginott, whose writings have inspired mine, certainly was not a prototypical midwesterner.) I hope, of course, that the content pertains to teachers working with young children in classrooms everywhere.

The chapters use words in particular ways to help explain the workings of guidance: *mistaken behavior, guidance talks, three levels of conflict management, the encouraging classroom, comprehensive guidance, liberation teaching.* You may be familiar already with some or all of these guidance concepts. You may be using them in your teaching now and have been for some time. If so, please accept these chapters as continuing encouragement for giving voice to what you are doing and who you are as a teacher. Especially if these ideas are new to you, and they help you reflect about how you are with children, then my response would be a definite grin.

The power of guidance, sometimes firm, but always friendly—"love does not always wear a smile"—resides in you. All in all, these chapters don't radiate quite as much humor as I would like—friendly humor enlightens guidance—but each one tells its own story and gives a particular perspective to the "power of guidance." I hope you will find these chapters empowering.

Best Wishes,
Dan Gartrell

PS: Readers can access handouts, tables, and forms on the Cengage Learning Web site at www.cengage.com/education
Click on the link for Online Resources™ where you will find the Online Resources™ to accompany *A Guidance Approach for the Encouraging Classroom, Third Edition* by Dan Gartrell. While this material accompanies Dan's textbook, much of it also has direct connection to ideas in this book.

ABOUT THE AUTHORS

Dan Gartrell has taught sixth grade in Ohio and Head Start for the Red Lake Band of Ojibwe in northern Minnesota. Dan received his Doctor of Education degree from the University of North Dakota in the late 1970s. He is director of the Child Development Training Program and professor of Early Childhood and Elementary Education at Bemidji State University. Dan is the author of many articles and two other books. He has done over 300 workshops in the areas of guidance, emergent literacy, and the development of intelligence. Dan is a member of a blended family that includes wife, Dr. Julie Jochum of Concordia University in St. Paul, five children aged 25 to 37, and nine [!] grandchildren. (He's got photos.) Dan can be reached at *dgartrell@bemidjistate.edu*

Nancy Weber, MA, resides in Bay City, Michigan, and has been presenting seminars, keynote speeches, and workshops since 1987. Nancy is a former classroom teacher, with over 25 years in the field of education, and has made over 1900 presentations for educators throughout the United States. She is co-author of *Teacher Talk: What It Really Means* and has worked as a film consultant for Disney Educational Productions. You may have read her story, "A Simple Touch," in the bestseller, *A Second Helping of Chicken Soup for the Soul*. Nancy and her husband, Jeffrey Taylor, DDS, have five nearly grown children. They enjoy raising and training hounds and other critters. Nancy can be reached at *nancyspeak@aol.com*

Margaret King received her Doctor of Education degree from the University of Massachusetts–Amherst. Margaret taught first and second grades in Freeport, New York. She was Director of the Ohio University Child Development Center for more than 15 years. Margaret also served as secretary and governing board member of NAEYC. She is currently professor of Early Childhood Teacher Education at Ohio University—Athens, working with the community as a change agent for improving early care and education experiences for young children and their families. Her current research focuses on boys. She lives in Athens, Ohio, with her 12-year-old son, Ross. Margaret can be reached at *kingm@ohio.edu*

Patience or Understanding?

By Nancy Weber

QUICK TAKE

When people hear that you are a teacher of young children, do they sometimes say, "You must be so patient"? What do you think when they say that? Nancy Weber, author of this short but thought-provoking chapter, answers the question for many early childhood professionals. I have always liked Nancy's answer, and am pleased she is letting us use her 1987 *Young Children* article to open the book. The first year that my own articles appeared in *Young Children* was 1987; a January article assailing assertive discipline, and a March article, accompanying Nancy's, entitled "Guidance or Punishment?" Of the three, Nancy's by far has the staying power—and sets the stage well for our exploration of the "power of guidance."

Ryan has just solved the problem of who will play with the kindergarten's only boy doll by punching five-year-old Nicky in the stomach.

Does Ryan's aggressive behavior try your patience? Is patience a desirable attribute for success in teaching young children? Will it help Ryan's teacher successfully deal with this situation? Just what does it mean to be patient?

Colleagues and the parents of my kindergarten students have often commented on the tremendous amounts of patience required to teach young children. "I'd never have the patience to work with little children." "Where do you get all that patience?" I found myself feeling increasingly uncomfortable with these compliments because I've never considered myself a very patient person.

Gradually, as I heard patience extolled by other teachers and in graduate courses, and saw it on attribute lists in teacher preparation textbooks, I began to question the concept of patience as a virtue. My discomfort with the concept of patience as an attribute of good teaching was explained when I looked up the term in *Webster's Dictionary.*

Patience is associated only with unpleasant situations and is not even considered in a pleasant context! Because I find teaching the young very pleasant, I now believe that patience is an *un*desirable teacher attribute; its presence (in large amounts at least) indicates a teacher who finds teaching unpleasant. I see myself as a successful teacher with very little patience. *Visitors to my classroom had mistakenly believed that I exhibited patience with young children, when in reality they were witnessing the behavior that results from understanding.*

> **Patience** is defined as "bearing pains or trials calmly or without complaint; manifesting forbearance under provocation or strain; steadfast despite opposition, difficulty, or adversity."

The teacher who understands the developmental level of the child does not need to "bear pains calmly." This teacher will accept behavior as developmentally appropriate and will not see the child as an adversary, because the child will be viewed as innately *good,* though inexperienced. Teachers who understand young children will see themselves as children's partners in learning and will not view the child as opposition. The adult will approach the learning situation and the child as a pleasure rather than a trial. The child's intuitive reaction to this approach will be positive and will create a positive learning experience.

A teacher's perceptions determine whether or not a particular circumstance requires patience. In my view, Ryan is not a naughty child, but a child with limited social skills. The aggressive behavior is understandable. To deal effectively with the situation, I must accept the physical aggression as appropriate to Ryan's level of development and social experience, but work to teach him other socially appropriate and effective behaviors. I might place my arms around both children while explaining (rather than reprimanding) that people must feel safe in school. "We may not hit people or hurt them. Next time use words to tell Nicky that you feel angry and want the doll back. Then Nicky will know what you want." *My perception is not that Ryan is interrupting my teaching, but that he is offering me an opportunity to model problem-solving skills, to create classroom discipline, and to encourage self-discipline.* The classroom scuffle offers me an opportunity to act as a learning enabler by helping Ryan and the other children learn how to meet basic safety and esteem needs. I do not want to depend on patience in order to act effectively, because each new circumstance will draw on my reserves. If I rely on patience, there is a danger of it running out, resulting in inappropriate teacher behaviors. If I rely on understanding, and this understanding is based on sound developmental theory, it will never run out.

Teachers who expect the kindergarten child to sit quietly while working, to form letters correctly, or to "keep your hands to yourself" will require patience because of a lack of understanding. Inappropriate demands create tension within teachers, within their young students, and between teacher and child. The teacher may demonstrate patience while calmly but tersely reminding, "Ryan, for the last time, take that pencil out of your mouth." Ryan may feel humiliated for unconsciously performing an act totally appropriate for a teething five- or six-year-old. If I understand, I will ignore the behavior or substitute a more suitable chewing material to satisfy the child's need. Nothing in my tone of voice, body language, or overall demeanor will indicate any tension of impatience, because I will not feel it. I understand.

Patience implies disrespect to the child because it is a condescending view that the patient person is somehow superior to the "opposition." It assumes that young children's behaviors provoke, oppose, and strain. This attitude contrasts with the developmental point of view of respect for the child's orderly, predictable development. Patient teachers perceive the aggressive child as the opponent, and are liable to set up an adversarial relationship in which they feel justifiably provoked into action against the child. In these power struggles, the teacher is the winner and the child always loses. The result may be the antithesis of the developmental point of view in the midst of a so-called "developmental" classroom: A child may be controlled instead of guided. She or he may be bullied into conformity rather than encouraged to develop uniqueness within social parameters. This teacher does not understand the child's needs and therefore cannot consider them. Impatience results when teachers are dominated by their own needs and cannot adequately take into account the needs of the child.

Teachers who understand young children know that they are not time-efficient. These teachers take time to trust in the natural growth process, to listen attentively, to respond descriptively and appreciatively. They take time to listen to what children are *unable* to say, as well as to expand upon what they *do* say. Such teachers make time to allow children to discover their world and build their reality through interactions with objects and people. When I understand, I accept that each child is worth all the time she or he needs. Because I accept what *is,* I put my energy into effective teaching, not into struggling against the reality that children are children.

A teacher who understands children's needs encourages growth. When basic physical and security needs are met in an accepting environment, children are able to risk growth and experience success. When love and belonging needs are met, the children are able to develop competence and self-acceptance. The satisfaction of esteem needs precludes acting out to gain the acceptance of peers and attention from the teacher. When I understand these needs, I search for ways to help children meet them. I encourage freedom, sharing, conversation, movement, risk-taking, and spontaneity—the natural characteristics of childhood. Children will struggle to use these capacities regardless of my attitude. They act to satisfy *their* needs, not the needs or goals of the teacher. Therefore, the teacher who works to satisfy the children's needs will be comfortable and successful in the teaching role. Children will feel comfortable with their natural, necessary activities and will not be subjected to feelings of inferiority imposed by an endlessly patient teacher.

Teachers rely on patience when their own basic needs are in conflict with the needs of their students. For example, children may need activity to meet basic physiological needs, but this may conflict with the teacher's physiological need (to avoid excessive noise), safety need (for a positive evaluation from an administrator), or esteem need (for peer approval). Meeting the children's needs is more likely to become the teacher's goal when she or he understands the developmental characteristics of early childhood. It is to be hoped that the teacher will then stop looking to children for the satisfaction of too many of the teacher's own needs and will concern herself or himself with the attainment of appropriate goals for each of the *children*. As an understanding professional, the teacher's own egocentrism will less likely interfere with educating the children, and she or he will be accepting of *their* egocentrism, an essential reality of very young children.

It is important for teachers to have mature healthy personalities because young children are very vulnerable and their development requires focused and sensitive nurturing. Teachers who have gone into early childhood education with their own basic needs unmet, or who feel oppressed and burdened, may inadvertently draw excessively from the children to meet their own basic needs. This preoccupation with concerns of their own precludes an understanding of children, and therefore makes *acting* upon this understanding impossible. Healthy teachers will look to their students for the fulfillment of self-actualization needs to enhance their lives *above and beyond* basics. This ensures an enriching interdependent growth experience for both.

An understanding professional values such attributes as organizational skills, problem-solving abilities, a broad knowledge base, and a thorough understanding of child development, and participates in activities to further these qualities. Graduate courses, membership in professional organizations, and consistent reading of professional journals will increase a teacher's understanding and implementation of current early childhood educational research and theory. Adult expectations will be appropriate to the developmental capabilities of the children and will encourage learning. Teachers will not define their own teaching abilities with unproductive terms like *patient,* but will articulate their role as professional educators in a legitimate field of study. While patient teachers are likely to see themselves as martyrs, struggling through days of adversity imposed by the children, professionals will celebrate *with* children the process of growth. Enthusiasm and joy can result as understanding teachers welcome student behaviors that patient teachers find irritating.

As early childhood educators work to validate their role as viable professionals—viable in the eyes of sometimes skeptical communities: administrators, upper-grade teachers, and parents—they must dispel the myth that patience is predominant in their success.

Parents and colleagues marvel at the early childhood teacher's patience *and* understanding. They misunderstand. Teachers possess patience *or* understanding: Patience is rarely necessary when one is understanding.

End Note: *This chapter was written by Nancy Weber and first appeared in the March, 1987 issue of* Young Children. *It is referenced as follows: Weber, N. (1987). Patience or understanding.* Young Children *42(3), 52–54.*

REFERENCES

Ames, L. B., & Ilg, F. L. (1979). *Your five-year-old.* New York: Dell.

Bloom, B. (1981). *All our children learning.* New York: McGraw-Hill.

Elkind, D. (1976). *Child development and education.* New York: Oxford University Press.

Maslow, A. H. (1954). *Motivation and personality.* New York: Harper & Row.

Moorman, C. (1985). *Talk sense to yourself.* Portage, Michigan: Personal Power Press.

Misbehavior or Mistaken Behavior?

QUICK TAKE

I always have had difficulty with the term **misbehavior.** For me, the cultural baggage of this term causes many teachers to make a moral judgment about a behavior and then make another moral judgment about the child. With their patience running out, these teachers too easily conclude that the "misbehaving" child needs to be "disciplined."

One explanation for this string of reactions is that these teachers have resorted to patience rather than understanding. They did not look into the situation to figure out: (1) reasons why the child behaved in a certain way, and (2) what they could teach so that the child can behave differently next time. These teachers have reacted to "misbehavior" in a way that prevented them from understanding the situation and taking a more positive course of action.

The term **mistaken behavior** encourages teachers to follow the two basic guidance practices above. Mistaken behavior reminds us that the child is just at the beginning of a lifelong learning process, which we also are undertaking, and that in the process of learning we all make mistakes. Some contend that the difference between misbehavior and mistaken behavior is semantic, two different terms that mean about the same thing. This chapter argues that there is a real difference between the terms, one that is made more clear by the distinction between patience and understanding. Knowing this difference gives teachers a guidance alternative for when classroom conflicts occur.

A common situation in early childhood classrooms is when two children argue over the use of a toy car. In this scenario two teachers handle the situation differently. *Teacher one* arrives, takes the car, and declares that because the children are not using it appropriately, they will have to find something else to do. One child sits on a chair and looks sad; the other child angrily sticks up an index finger at the teacher's back as she puts the car on the shelf (Gartrell, 2003).

Teacher two arrives, gets down on the children's level and holds the car. She says, "We have a problem. There is one car and two children want to play with it. Please use your words so we can solve this problem." With a bit of coaching, the two children determine that one child had the car first and the other wanted it. The teacher then helps the second child find "an almost new car that no one is using." The children play together using the two cars.

TRADITIONAL CLASSROOM DISCIPLINE VERSUS CONFLICT RESOLUTION AND GUIDANCE

In their responses, the first teacher used traditional classroom discipline; the second used conflict resolution (Wichert, 1989), an important technique in guidance. As commonly practiced, traditional discipline has failed to distinguish between nonpunitive teacher intervention and punishment (Gartrell, 1987; Reynolds, 1990). The effects of punishment—diminished self-esteem, loss of enjoyment of learning, negative feelings toward self and others—make its use inappropriate in the classroom setting (Bredekamp, 1987).

The difference between these two approaches is that traditional discipline criticizes children—often publicly—for unacceptable behaviors, whereas guidance teaches children positive alternatives, "what they can do instead." Traditional discipline punishes children for having problems they cannot solve, while guidance teaches children to solve their problems in socially acceptable ways (Gartrell, 2003).

One of the joys of teaching young children, despite a continuing lack of resources in the early childhood field, is the capacity of the professional to be fully nurturing within the teaching role. The practice of guidance, the creation and maintenance of a positive learning environment for each child, supports the nurturing function. Guidance connotes activism on the teacher's part (Gartrell, 2003). The teacher who uses guidance is not permissive; she or he does not let children struggle vis-à-vis boundaries that may not be there. Instead, the teacher provides leadership so that children can interact successfully within the reasonable boundaries of the classroom community.

"MISBEHAVIOR" MAKES US THINK OF PUNISHING

As classroom guidance continues to displace a reliance on traditional discipline, it is important that educators reevaluate other widely used terms and practices. As discussed, one such term is misbehavior. Traditionally, misbehavior implies willful wrongdoing for which a child must be disciplined (punished). The term invites moral labeling of the child. After all, what kind of children misbehave? Children who are "naughty," "rowdy," "mean," "willful," "not nice." Although teachers who punish misbehavior believe they are "shaming children into being good," the result may be the opposite. Because of limited development and experience, children tend to internalize negative labels, see themselves as they are labeled, and react accordingly (Ginott, 1975).

Greenberg (1988) makes the point that informed early childhood teachers do not think in terms of good or bad children but good or bad forms of discipline. When children act out, there are more important things to do than criticize the supposed character flaws of the child or fuss about the specific method of discipline to use. The teacher needs to consider the reasons for the behavior—was it a mismatch of the child and the curriculum, for instance, or trouble in the child's life outside school?

Equally important, the teacher needs to think about how to teach the child acceptable alternatives during and after the intervention. Many teachers of young children try to follow the prescription of Ginott: address the behavior; protect the personality (1975). As long as the teacher views mistaken acts as misbehavior, however, the avoidance of punishment and labeling becomes difficult, because of the moralistic baggage that the term carries (Gartrell, 2003).

Probably the roots of the term misbehavior go back to the Middle Ages and the view that children, by nature, were "wayward" and "tending toward evil" (Osborn, 1980). Historically, "beating the devil" out of children for misbehavior has been an accepted teaching practice. Berger (1991) and especially deMause (1974) establish that strict discipline, based on obedience and corporal punishment, was common in schools into the 20th century. With modern permutations, "obedience or consequences" discipline still persists in schools today—to control children's misbehavior.

MISTAKEN BEHAVIOR MAKES US THINK OF GUIDING AND EDUCATING

In European-American education, a moralistic attitude about the nature of children has been common. Another viewpoint has coexisted, however, that children have worth in and of themselves and, with guidance, tend toward good (Osborn, 1980). Since the middle of the last century, this more benevolent perspective has manifested itself in the work of such educators and psychologists as Froebel, Montessori, Dewey, Piaget, Purkey, Ginott, and all major modern early childhood educators (Gartrell, 2003). Common in the writings of these progressives are the ideas that

- the child is in a state of development.
- the processes of learning and developing are complex.
- through methods and curriculum, educators need to accommodate the developmental and experiential circumstances of each child.
- guiding behavior is a big part of every teacher's job.

Certainly, this is the premise of the well-known 1987 [revised 1997] National Association for the Education of Young Children (NAEYC) position statement on developmentally appropriate practice.

In her article "Avoiding 'Me Against You' Discipline," Greenberg (1988) frames the issue of teacher-child relations from the developmental perspective:

> Some adults see each individual child as being at this moment "good" and at that moment "bad." It all adds up to a view of a child as, overall, either a "good child" or a "bad child": She's a good girl; he's a hateful child, a really naughty boy.

> Other adults, and certainly those of us well educated in child development, think differently about children. We consider all infants, toddlers, and young children potentially good people, naive little people with a very small amount of experience on Earth, who have much to learn, and a great deal of motivation to please, to be accepted, to be approved, to be loved, to be cared for. We see young children as generally receptive to guidance and usually eager to "do it right." (pp. 24–25)

In the process of learning the complex life skills of cooperation, conflict resolution, and acceptable expression of strong feelings, children, like all of us, make mistakes (Gartrell, 1987). The guidance tradition in early childhood education suggests that teachers who traditionally have considered problems in the classroom as misbehaviors think of them instead as mistaken behaviors (MnAEYC, 1991). By considering behaviors as mistaken, the teacher is freed from the impediment of moral judgment about the child and empowered instead to meditate, problem-solve, and guide.

In the cognitive domain, a child who asks, "Is him going, too, teacher?" is not treated as though she has misbehaved. In an affirming manner, the teacher models the conventional usage, "Yes, Carlita, he is going, too." In the realm of behavior, the teacher also uses a positive approach. Children are not punished for the mistakes of words or deeds; they are helped to learn from their mistaken behavior. The concept of mistaken behavior fits well with the guidance approach.

Children's behavior poses higher emotional stakes for the teacher than most other teaching situations (Gartrell, 2003). Matters of potential harm, disruption, and loss of control (by the adult as well as the child) are involved. This urgency factor makes accepting of the concept of mistaken behavior difficult for some teachers. The issue of intentionality also poses questions about the concept. If a child does something on purpose, is it still a mistaken behavior? The remainder of this chapter examines the concept of mistaken behavior.

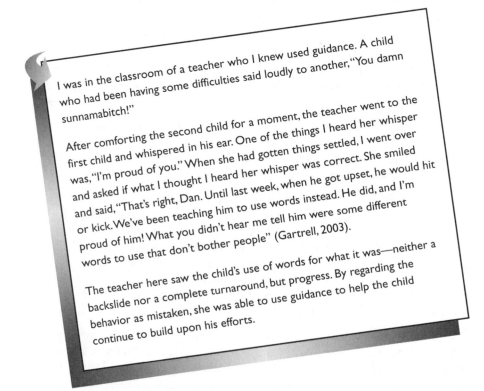

I was in the classroom of a teacher who I knew used guidance. A child who had been having some difficulties said loudly to another, "You damn sunnamabitch!"

After comforting the second child for a moment, the teacher went to the first child and whispered in his ear. One of the things I heard her whisper was, "I'm proud of you." When she had gotten things settled, I went over and asked if what I thought I heard her whisper was correct. She smiled and said, "That's right, Dan. Until last week, when he got upset, he would hit or kick. We've been teaching him to use words instead. He did, and I'm proud of him! What you didn't hear me tell him were some different words to use that don't bother people" (Gartrell, 2003).

The teacher here saw the child's use of words for what it was—neither a backslide nor a complete turnaround, but progress. By regarding the behavior as mistaken, she was able to use guidance to help the child continue to build upon his efforts.

ORIGINS OF THE TERM *MISTAKEN BEHAVIOR*

Over the past 30 years, Rudolph Dreikurs (1968; Dreikurs, Grunwald, & Pepper, 1982) has added much to our thinking about behavior management. Dreikurs's ideas, with which many readers are probably familiar, have been stepping-stones to the concept of mistaken behavior. Dreikurs postulated that all behavior is purposeful, and the purpose of behavior is to achieve social acceptance. Dreikurs derived four goals of misbehavior: attention getting, power seeking, revenge seeking, and displaying inadequacy (1968). Usually pursued by the child in order, the four goals represent inappropriate ways of seeking social acceptance. *Dreikurs's landmark contribution was that he suggested nonmoralizing intervention strategies, such as "logical consequences," to correct children's behavior* (1968). He spoke of the importance of democratic leadership in the classroom—the need for teachers to earn, rather than try to force, respect (Dreikurs, 1968). For educators and parents alike, Dreikurs has done much to raise the discussion of behavior above the level of moralization.

As important as his contributions are, Dreikurs wrote before recent findings surfaced about child development. As well, his views differ, in part, from those of the "self" psychologists of the 1960s and 1970s—Maslow, Rogers, Combs, Purkey, and others (Gartrell, 2003). For Dreikurs, social acceptance was the primary motivation in children's behavior. In contrast, both developmental and self psychologists see social acceptance as a foundation for full, balanced personal development rather than as an end in itself.

The concept of mistaken behavior draws from Dreikurs's nonmoralizing approach but draws more directly from the developmental and self psychologists. The concept of *mistaken* behavior, rather than misbehavior is an extension of the work of Steven Harlow (1975). Harlow integrated the thinking of Piaget, Erikson, Holt, and Riesman in his construct of *relational patterns.* Harlow (1975) explains, "By relational patterns, I mean ways in which children relate to situations, persons, and things in the school environment" (p. 28).

Harlow writes about three levels of relational patterns, "which differ in their openness to experience, maturity, and their capacity to operate freely" (p. 28). The three levels are survival, adjustment, and encountering. Children may show different relational patterns in different situations. Harlow cautions against using such behavioral constructs in order to label; instead, the purpose is to help children progress in their personal and social development.

THREE LEVELS OF MISTAKEN BEHAVIOR

From almost 30 years of teaching and observing in early childhood classrooms, I have identified three levels of mistaken behavior, based on Harlow's writings (Gartrell, 1987, 2003). As Table 2–1 illustrates, the levels

TABLE 2–1

Common Sources of Motivation
Relational Patterns and Levels of Mistaken Behavior

Motivational Source	Relational Pattern	Level of Mistaken Behavior
Desire to explore the environment and engage in relationships and activities	Encounterer	One: Experimentation
Desire to please and identify with significant others	Adjustor	Two: Socially influenced
Inability to cope with problems resulting from health conditions and life experiences	Survivor	Three: Strong needs

of mistaken behavior share motivational sources with the relational patterns. The levels of mistaken behavior identify the types of problems children in the various relational patterns are likely to experience.

Level Three:
Strong-Needs Mistaken Behavior

Children showing the survival relational pattern likely have experienced their environment as a "dangerous and painful place" over which they have little control (Harlow, 1975). The behavior patterns of these children tend to be rigid and exaggerated. To protect themselves, they resist change and continue the same behaviors in new situations, even if their patterns are extreme and inappropriate.

The child at the survival level is difficult for teachers to accept because of the nonsocial, at times antisocial, character of the child's behavior. Yet it is necessary for the teacher to establish a productive relationship, built on trust, in order to empower the child to progress to a higher relational level.

Children at the survival relational pattern show *Level Three, strong-needs mistaken behavior.* Wherever it occurs, this level of mistaken behavior is the most serious. A sure sign that the mistaken behavior is at Level Three is that it continues over time. (Anyone, including teachers, can have an occasional Level Three day.) As Harlow suggests, strong-needs mistaken behavior results from psychological and/or physical pain in the child's life that is beyond the child's ability to cope with and understand. Often children show strong-needs mistaken behavior in the classroom because it is a safe haven in their environment. Through withdrawal or acting out, these children are asking for help in the only way they can (Gartrell, 2003).

As the most serious level of mistaken behavior, the teacher takes a comprehensive approach with the child that usually involves other adults, especially parents or caregivers. The teacher

- intervenes nonpunitively.
- works to build a positive relationship with the child.
- seeks more information through observation.
- seeks more information through conversation with the child, other adults who work with the child, and parents or caregivers.
- creates a coordinated "individual guidance plan" in consultation with the other adults.
- implements, reviews, and modifies the plan as necessary. (Gartrell, 2003)

Sometimes Level Three mistaken behaviors are symptoms of such deep problems in the child's life that the comprehensive guidance approach is not completely successful. Even when working with parents, the teacher cannot necessarily change life circumstances for a child, but she or he can make life easier—in ways that may have lasting beneficial effects.

Level Two:
Socially Influenced Mistaken Behavior

Children who show the adjustment relational pattern have an increased ability to adapt to situations. Their criteria for doing so, however, is the judgment of significant others. "New ways of thinking and behaving are first sanctioned by an individual or reference group representing authority, before they are considered by the adjustor" (Harlow, 1975, p. 30). Children at the adjustment level seek high levels of teacher approval, put off completing tasks because "I can't do it right," and may involve adults or other children in doing their projects for them. They lack the self-esteem and individual strength necessary to respond to a situation on its own terms.

Some teachers find gratification in the obedience and dependence of a child at the adjustment level. They may be reinforcing long-term, other-directed response tendencies in the child, however, that inhibit full personal development (Harlow, 1975). Deprived of confidence in his own values and judgment, the child may continue to be influenced by others— especially peers—including toward self-destructive or oppressive mistaken behaviors (Gartrell, 2003). With a child at the adjustment level, the task of the teacher is to nudge him or her toward autonomy (the encountering relational pattern) by helping the child build self-esteem and proactive social skills (Harlow, 1975).

Children showing the adjustment relational pattern are subject to *Level Two, socially influenced mistaken behavior.* Level Two mistaken behaviors are "learned behaviors," reinforced in the child, intentionally or unintentionally, by other people important in the child's life. A child who uses an expletive in a classroom exactly as an adult would is showing a socially influenced mistaken behavior. Likewise, children who join others in calling a child "poopy butt" or "dorky" have been influenced by peers into a Level Two mistaken behavior.

In responding to Level Two mistaken behaviors, the teacher notes whether one child or a group of children are involved. When a group of children are involved, an effective technique, even with preschoolers (Hendrick, 1992), is the class meeting. Respecting the dignity of all concerned, the teacher points out the problem and, with the children, works out a solution. The teacher monitors progress and calls additional meetings, if necessary. If one child is involved, the teacher handles the situation privately; in a firm but friendly manner, explains what is unacceptable; and provides a guideline for an acceptable alternative. In either individual or group situations, the teacher follows up with encouragement and "compliment sandwiches"—two or three acknowledgments of progress along with one reminder of the agreed-to guideline (Gartrell, 2003) (it is easier for us to change behaviors when others acknowledge our efforts).

By assisting children to learn alternatives to socially influenced mistaken behavior, the teacher helps them to understand that they have the capacity to evaluate, choose, and interact for themselves—essential life skills for a democracy (Wittmer & Honig, 1994).

Level One:
Experimentation Mistaken Behavior

Harlow's construct of relational patterns is built around the importance of autonomy—Piaget's term for the ability of the individual to make intelligent, ethical decisions (Kamii, 1984). Autonomy is the social relation pattern shown by children at the highest level, *encountering* (Harlow, 1975).

Children at the encountering level are learning most effectively about themselves and the world; yet, because they are so open to new experience and because they are young, they are susceptible to mistaken behavior—and vulnerable to teacher criticism. About children at the encountering level, Harlow (1975) states:

> In contrast with the adjustor and survivor, the encounterer is less concerned with security and certainty and much more occupied with what Erikson referred to as the inner mechanism that permits the individual to turn "passive into active" and to maintain and regain in this world of contending forces an individual sense of centrality, of wholeness, and of initiative. (pp. 30–31)

Children at the encountering relational pattern show *Level One, experimentation mistaken behavior.* The term **experimentation** is used because the child is learning through full engagement in the experiment of life. To cite previous illustrations, the two children who argued over the use of a toy car were totally involved in that situation; they were demonstrating Level One mistaken behavior. Interestingly, perhaps in progressing from Level Three, the child who swore rather then hit also was showing Level One mistaken behavior. The experimentation can be "natural," through full involvement in the affairs of the classroom, or it can be "controlled," as in the case of a young child who, with a smile, uses an expletive in order to see the teacher's reaction.

The teacher responds in different ways to different situations. Sometimes he or she may step back and allow a child to learn from the experience; other times, the teacher will reiterate a guideline and, in a friendly tone, teach a more appropriate alternative behavior. With children at Level One, as with those at Two and Three, the teacher uses guidance and avoids the use of traditional discipline.

UNDERSTANDING MISTAKEN BEHAVIORS

An occasional misunderstanding about mistaken behavior is that some mistaken behaviors occur at only Level One, others at Level Two, and still others at Level Three (Gartrell, 2003). At each level, mistaken behaviors have distinct motivational sources. Behaviors that appear similar can be a result of differing motivations, and so be at different levels. The teacher must observe carefully to infer the motivation and the level of mistaken behavior in order to respond effectively. Table 2–2 illustrates how similar mistaken behaviors can be at different levels.

At any relational level, the cause of mistaken behavior is insufficient understanding about how to act maturely in the complex situations of life. With a child's internal need to go forward and to learn—but limited ability to balance his or her own needs with those of others—mistaken behavior will occur. Knowledge of the relational patterns and the levels of mistaken behavior assists the teacher to understand and work with children when they make mistakes (Gartrell, 2003).

THE ISSUE OF INTENTIONALITY

When people think about behavior, they may associate mistaken behavior with "accidents" and misbehavior with acts "done on purpose" (Gartrell, 2003). Mistaken behavior includes both accidents and intentional behaviors. A young child on a trike who runs over the toe of another child by accident has shown Level One mistaken behavior. The

TABLE 2 – 2

Sample Mistaken Behaviors by Level

Incident of Mistaken Behavior	Motivational Source	Level of Mistaken Behavior
Child uses expletive	Wants to see teacher's reaction	One
	Emulates important others	Two
	Expresses deeply felt hostility	Three
Child takes ball from another child	Wants ball; has not learned to ask in words	One
	Follows aggrandizement practices modeled by other children	Two
	Feels need to act out against world by asserting power	Three
Child refuses to join in group activity	Does not understand teacher's expectations	One
	Has developed a habit of not joining in	Two
	Is not feeling well or feels anxiety about participating	Three

accident was unintentional but was Level One because it was a mistake that arose from involvement.

A child may run over another's foot for a second reason related to Level One (Gartrell, 2003). As a part of encountering social relations, the trike rider hits the other's foot "accidentally on purpose" to see what will happen. The lack of development of young children results in their difficulty understanding how another child would feel under such circumstances. The act was intentional but was done without full awareness of the consequences and so is Level One mistaken behavior. The importance of the term *mistaken behavior* is that it reminds the adult that the trike rider needs guidance about human feelings and the consequences of actions, not punishment for making a mistake.

Of course, hitting another child's foot might also be a Level Two or Level Three mistaken behavior (Gartrell, 2003). At Level Two, one child follows another on a trike. The second rider sees the first swing close to a bystander and follows suit but strikes the bystander's foot. At Level Three, a trike rider who is harboring feelings of hostility acts out against an innocent child. When the teacher hypothesizes that Level Two or Level Three is involved, she reacts with increasing degrees of firmness, although she retains the element of friendliness, which is at the heart of guidance. If the trike rider's motives indicate that strong-needs mistaken behavior is present, the teacher should follow up as suggested for Level Three. The additional step is important because serious mistaken behaviors occur when children are the victims of life circumstances that are beyond their control. Even the mistaken behavior of aggression is a non-verbal request for assistance, not a situation requiring punishment.

It should be noted that whatever the level of mistaken behavior, the teacher reacts to the immediate situation by using guidance. The teacher first gives attention to the victim, who deserves it. This action shows support for the wronged child (and also may help the teacher calm down). The teacher then speaks with the trike rider. She does some empathy building by pointing out that the trike hurt the other child and she cannot let anyone (including the trike rider) be hurt at school. She discusses with the trike rider how he could avoid having this problem next time. Although the teacher does not force an apology, she perhaps asks how the trike rider could help the child who was hurt feel better. The teacher then assists the trike rider back into positive activity, which often includes helping him to make amends. In guidance practice the teacher avoids the traditional discipline reaction. She does not lecture about how naughty the behavior was or automatically put the child in a time-out. The goal is to help the child learn from the mistake, not punish him for making it.

Again, the value of the term *mistaken behavior* is that it has different implications than the conventional term, *misbehavior.* Misbehavior tends to connote a judgment of character that leads to punishment rather than guidance. Mistaken behavior precludes character assessment and asks that the child be accepted as a person of worth (by virtue of being alive). The person may need to face consequences, but at the base of those consequences is guidance, so the possibility of change is maximized (Gartrell, 2003).

A premise in the use of guidance is that even willful acts that are done "on purpose" still constitute mistaken behavior. A child who deliberately bites or intentionally disobeys has made a mistake. The adult who is able to approach children as worthwhile individuals who make mistakes is in a philosophically strong position to assist them with healthy personal and social development.

End Note: *This chapter first appeared in the July 1995 issue of* Young Children. *It is referenced as follows: Gartrell, D. J. (1995). Misbehavior or Mistaken Behavior?* Young Children *50(5), 27–34.*

REFERENCES

Berger, S. K. (1991). *The developing person through childhood and adolescence.* New York: Worth.

Bredekamp, S.(Ed.). (1987). *Developmentally appropriate practice in early childhood programs serving children from birth through age 8* (Exp. ed.). Washington, DC: NAEYC.

Bredekamp, S., & Copple, C.(Eds.). (1997). *Developmentally appropriate practice in early childhood programs* (Rev. ed.). Washington, DC: NAEYC.

deMause, L.(Ed.). (1974). *The history of childhood.* New York: Peter Benrick Books.

Dreikurs, R.(1968). *Psychology in the classroom* (2nd ed.). New York: Harper & Row.

Dreikurs, R., Grunwald, B., & Pepper, F.(1982). *Maintaining sanity in the classroom.* New York: Harper and Row Publishers.

Gartrell, D. J. (1987). More thoughts . . . Punishment or guidance? *Young Children 42* (3), 55–61.

Gartrell, D. J. (2003). *A guidance approach for the encouraging classroom (3rd ed).* Clifton Park, NY: Delmar Learning.

Ginott, H. G. (1975). *Teacher and child.* New York: Avon Books.

Greenberg, P.(1988). Ideas that work with young children. Avoiding "me against you" discipline. *Young Children 44* (1), 24–29.

Harlow, S. D. (1975). *Special education: The meeting of differences.* Grand Forks, ND: University of North Dakota.

Hendrick, J.(1992). Where does it all begin? Teaching the principles of democracy in the early years. *Young Children 47* (3), 51–53.

Kamii, C.(1984). Autonomy: The aim of education envisioned by Piaget. *Phi Delta Kappan 65*(6), 410–415.

Minnesota Association for the Education of Young Children (MnAEYC). (1991). *Developmentally appropriate guidance of children birth to eight* (Rev. ed.). St. Paul: Author.

Osborn, D. K. (1980). *Early childhood education in historical perspective.* Athens, GA: Education Associates.

Reynolds, E.(1990). *Guiding young children: A child-centered approach.* Mountain View, CA: Mayfield.

Wichert, S.(1989). *Keeping the peace: Practicing cooperation and conflict resolution with preschoolers.* Philadelphia: New Society.

Wittmer, D. S., & Honig, A. S. (1994). Encouraging positive social development in young children. *Young Children 49* (5), 61–75.

CHAPTER 3

Beyond Discipline to Guidance

The word *discipline* has a noble root that means "instruction" or "training." The problem is that in European-American classrooms hundreds of years of harsh punishment in the name of discipline has tainted the term. To illustrate, the accepted modern meaning of "to discipline a child" is to punish. The first two chapters encouraged teachers to modify their perspectives from being *patient* to being *understanding* and from seeing *misbehavior* to recognizing *mistaken behavior.* Chapter Three argues that it is also time to replace the practice of "discipline" with *guidance.*

Many readers already make this mental adjustment by adding an adjective like "positive" to discipline. Whatever terms are used, teachers need to reject discipline practices that lapse into punishment. The message of Chapter Three is that we can teach the social-emotional skills children need to function as healthy and productive adults in consistently positive ways. We can even teach these skills when children show strong-needs mistaken behavior. When we do so—helping children to solve their problems rather than punishing children for having problems they cannot solve—teachers are practicing not traditional discipline, but guidance.

Krista Anderson, a student teacher in a Head Start classroom, recorded in her journal an anecdotal observation of two children involved in a confrontation (reprinted with permission); the children here are named Charissa and Carlos.

OBSERVATION

Charissa and Carlos were building with blocks. Charissa reached for a block, and Carlos decided he wanted the same one. They both tugged on the block, and then Carlos hit Charissa on the back. Charissa fought back tears and said, "Carlos, you're not s'posed to hit—you're s'posed to use the 'talking stick.' "

Carlos said yeah and got the stick. I couldn't hear what they said, but they took turns holding the stick and talking while the other one listened. After only a minute, the two were playing again, and Charissa was using the block. Later I asked her what the talking stick helped them decide. She said, "That I use the block first this time. Carlos uses it next time."

REFLECTION

I really got concerned when Carlos hit Charissa, and I was just about to get involved. I couldn't believe it when Charissa didn't hit back but told Carlos to get the talking stick—and he did! Then they solved the problem so quickly. DeeAnn [the teacher] told me she has been teaching the kids since September [it was now April] to solve their problems by using the talking stick. Usually she has to mediate, but this time two children solved a problem on their own. It really worked!

Preschoolers do not typically solve a problem like this, on their own, by using a prop like a talking stick! But DeeAnn had been working with the children all year to teach them this conflict management skill. To ensure consistency, she had persuaded the other adults in the room to also use the talking stick (even once themselves!). Utilizing the ideas of

Wichert (1989), the adults started by using a lot of coaching (high-level mediation) but over time encouraged the children to take the initiative to solve their problems themselves.

Conflict management—in this case through the technique of a decorated, venerable talking stick—is an important strategy in the overall approach to working with children, called guidance (Janke & Penshorn Peterson, 1995). By now guidance is a familiar term in early childhood education, as is its companion term, developmentally appropriate practice (DAP). However, like the misinterpretations of DAP that have surfaced over the years, some interpretations of guidance show a misunderstanding of what the approach is about. Erroneous interpretations have led to the misapplication of guidance ideas: some teachers may think they are using guidance when they are not.

This chapter is an effort to clarify the concept of guidance. It defines guidance, traces the guidance tradition in early childhood education, examines the present trend toward guidance, explains what guidance is not, and illustrates key practices in classrooms where teachers use guidance.

GUIDANCE DEFINED

Teachers who practice guidance believe in the positive potential of children, manifest through a dynamic process of development (Greenberg, 1988). For this reason, teachers who use guidance think beyond conventional classroom discipline—the intent of which is to keep children (literally and figuratively) in line. Rather than simply being a reaction to crises, guidance involves developmentally appropriate, culturally responsive education to reduce the occurrence of classroom problems. Guidance means creating a positive learning environment for each child in the group.

Guidance teaches children the life skills they need as citizens of a democracy (Wittmer & Honig, 1994): respecting others and one's self, working together in groups, solving problems using words, expressing strong emotions in acceptable ways, and making decisions ethically and intelligently. Teachers who use guidance realize that it takes well into adulthood to master these skills and that, in learning them, children—like all of us—make mistakes. Therefore, because children are just beginning this personal development, teachers regard behaviors traditionally considered misbehaviors as mistaken behaviors (Gartrell 1987b, 1995). The interventions teachers make to address mistaken behaviors are firm, but friendly, instructive and solution oriented, but not punitive. The teacher helps children learn from their mistakes rather than punishing them for the mistakes they make; empowers children to solve problems rather than punishing them for having problems they cannot solve; and helps children accept consequences, but consequences that teach and leave self-esteem intact rather than punish.

Guidance teaching is character education in its truest, least political sense—guiding children to develop the empathy, self-esteem, and self-control needed for autonomy, Piaget's term for the capacity to make intelligent, ethical decisions (Kamii, 1984). In contrast to the notion that the teacher handles all problem situations alone, guidance involves teamwork with professionals and partnerships with parents on behalf of the child.

THE GUIDANCE TRADITION

Educators interested in social reform long have viewed children as being in a state of dynamic development and adults as patterning effective education and guidance practices responsive to the developmental pattern of the child. During the 19th century the European educators Herbart, Pestalozzi, and Froebel began fundamental educational reform, in no small part as a result of their views on the child's dynamic nature (Osborn, 1980).

German born Friedrich Froebel was the originator of the kindergarten, at the time intended for children aged three to six. Froebel incorporated such practices as manipulatives-based instruction, circle time, home visits, "mothers' meetings," and the use of women teachers (Lilley, 1967). For Froebel the whole purpose of education was guidance so that the "innate impulses of the child" could be developed harmoniously through creative activity. As part of his early developmental orientation, Froebel believed that the nature of the child was essentially good and that "faults" were the product of negative experiences, sometimes at the hand of the educator (Lilley, 1967).

Similarly, Maria Montessori took a developmental viewpoint, maintaining that "the child is in a continual state of growth and metamorphosis, whereas the adult has reached the norm of the species" (cited in Standing, 1962, p. 106). Montessori—as well as her American contemporary, John Dewey—abhorred the traditional schooling of the day, which failed to consider children's development. She criticized didactic teaching practices with children planted behind desks, expected to recite lessons of little meaning in their lives, and kept in line by systematic rewards and punishments (Montessori, 1964). Her approach made the child an active agent in the education process; through this responsibility children would learn self-discipline.

Like Montessori, Dewey viewed discipline as differing in method depending on the curriculum followed. The "preprimary" level in Dewey's University of Chicago Laboratory School featured project-based learning activities that built from the everyday experience of the young learners. In his 1900 monograph *The School and Society,* Dewey states:

If you have the end in view of forty or fifty children learning certain set lessons, to be recited to the teacher, your discipline must be devoted to securing that result. But if the end in view is the development of a spirit of social co-operation and community life, discipline must grow out of and be relative to such an aim. There is a certain disorder in any busy workshop; there is not silence; persons are not engaged in maintaining certain fixed physical postures; their arms are not folded; they are not holding their books thus and so. They are doing a variety of things, and there is the confusion, the bustle that results from activity. Out of the occupation, out of doing things that are to produce results, and out of doing these in a social and co-operative way, there is born a discipline of its own kind and type. Our whole conception of discipline changes when we get this point of view. (1969, pp. 16–17)

Dewey, of course, was not just speaking of early childhood education but of schooling at all levels. Almost 100 years later, his words still challenge America's educators and eloquently capture the "guidance difference."

Midcentury Influences

In the first half of the 20th century, progressive educators and psychologists increasingly viewed children not in traditional moralistic terms (good and bad) but in terms responsive to a positive developmental potential. The nursery school movement in Britain and the United States was imbued with these progressive ideas and influenced the writings of two midcentury early childhood educators, James L. Hymes Jr. (1949, 1955) and Katherine Read (1950).

Katherine Read Baker was a nursery education leader. Her classic *The Nursery School: A Human Relations Laboratory* (1950) outlines a view of the classroom as a supportive environment for both children and adults to gain understanding in the challenging area of human relationships. Read speaks clearly of the child's need for understandable, consistent limits and of the use of authority to encourage self-control:

Our goal is self-control, the only sound control. But self-control can be sound only when there is a stable mature self. Our responsibility is to help the child develop maturity through giving him the security of limits maintained by responsible adults while he is growing. ([1950] 1993, p. 233)

Hymes distinguished himself as director of the noted Kaiser Day Care Centers during World War II and later as one of the people who strongly influenced the educational approach basic to Head Start. Hymes wrote frequently about early childhood education matters, including the landmark *Effective Home-School Relations* (1953). His *Discipline* (1949) and *Behavior and Misbehavior* (1955) stressed the importance of understanding the reasons for children's behavior. He argued that the causes of problems often are not in the child alone but a result of the program placing inappropriate developmental expectations on the child.

Hymes and Read both stressed the need for teachers to have high expectations of children—but expectations in line with each child's development. They articulated a key guidance premise, that the teacher must be willing to modify the daily program for the benefit of children, not just hold the program as a fixed commodity, against which the behavior of the child is to be judged. The basic educational and child guidance philosophy of Head Start, which was created as a nationwide program by War on Poverty leaders in 1965, was the nursery school/kindergarten philosophy developed long before and taught to several generations of teachers by Read, Hymes, and others of like persuasion.

Jean Piaget, often considered the preeminent developmental psychologist of the 20th century, discussed implications of his work for the classroom in *The Moral Judgment of the Child* (1932/1960). The Swiss psychologist shared with Montessori the precept that children learn through constructing knowledge by interacting with the environment. Further, he shared with Dewey and leaders of nursery school and kindergarten education a high regard for the social context of learning—insisting that peer interaction is essential for healthy development. He maintained that education must be an interactive endeavor and that discipline must respect and respond to this fact. Speaking directly about the uses of conventional classroom discipline, Piaget points out:

> If one thinks of the systematic resistance offered by pupils to the authoritarian method, and the admirable ingenuity employed by children the world over to evade disciplinary constraint, one cannot help regarding as defective a system which allows so much effort to be wasted instead of using it in cooperation. (1932/1960, pp. 366–367)

Like Dewey, Read, and Hymes, Piaget saw the classroom as a "laboratory" in which the practice of democracy was to be modeled, taught, and learned. For these writers, the means to social, personal, and intellectual development was guidance practiced in the classroom by a responsible adult.

As Piaget's work demonstrates, midcentury psychologists as well as educators have enhanced guidance ideas. Two such psychologists are Dreikurs (1968) and Ginott (1972). In line with Adler's theory about personality development, Dreikurs's construct of Mistaken Goals of Behavior has contributed to the present concept of mistaken behavior. Ginott, a particular influence on my writing, has contributed much to the language of guidance, illustrated by one of his more famous quotes: "To reach a child's mind, a teacher must capture his heart. Only if a child feels right can he think right" (1972, p. 69). Across the middle of the century, a broad array of educators and psychologists nurtured and sustained the guidance tradition.

The 1980s

Through the 1970s the guidance tradition was sustained by writers such as Jeannette Galambos Stone (1978) and Rita Warren (1977), who authored widely read monographs for the National Association for the Education of Young Children (NAEYC), along with many other well-known early childhood educators. While guidance was becoming important in preschool programs, a new trend in the public schools threatened to stop the percolating of guidance ideas, a long-sought goal of early childhood educators. "Back to the basics" became the call of public school educators, and curriculum and teaching methods grew more proscribed. During this time academic and disciplinary constraints were even put on kindergarten and preschool children. With disregard for young children's development, teachers were pressured to "get students ready" for the academics of the next level—a pressure still felt by some early childhood teachers today.

During these years, the interactive nature of the guidance approach did not fit the regiment of the academic classroom. New "obedience-driven" discipline systems, such as assertive discipline, came into widespread use at all levels of public education—and even in some preschool programs (Gartrell, 1987a; Hitz, 1988). In *Discipline with Dignity,* Curwin and Mendler lamented the widespread adoption of obedience models of discipline by public schools:

> It is ironic that the current mood of education is in some ways behind the past. The 1980s might someday be remembered as the decade when admiration was reserved for principals, cast as folk heroes walking around schools with baseball bats, and for teachers and whole schools that systematically embarrassed students by writing their names on the chalkboard. But we do have hope that the pendulum will once again swing to the rational position of treating children as people with needs and feelings that are not that different from adults. Once we begin to understand how obedience is contrary to the goals of our culture and education, the momentum will begin to shift. Our view is that the highest virtue of education is to teach students to be self-responsible and fully functional. In all but extreme cases, obedience contradicts these goals. (1988, p. 24)

THE GUIDANCE TREND

Throughout the 1980s and up to the present, educators and writers at the early childhood level maintained their independence from the obedience emphasis in conventional discipline. In 1987 NAEYC published its expanded *Developmentally Appropriate Practice in Early Childhood Programs Serving Children from Birth through Age 8* (Bredekamp, 1987).

Now in its revised edition (Bredekamp & Copple, 1997), the position statement and document advocate the interactive teaching practices responsive to the development of each child that our profession has always had. In relation to behavior management, the document reflects the guidance approach and draws a sharp distinction with conventional elementary school classroom discipline. In *appropriate* teaching practices,

> Teachers facilitate the development of social skills, self-control, and self-regulation in children by using positive guidance techniques, such as modeling and encouraging expected behavior, redirecting children to more acceptable activities, setting clear limits, and intervening to enforce consequences for unacceptable, harmful behavior. Teachers' expectations respect children's developing capabilities. Teachers are patient, realizing that not every minor infraction warrants a response. (Bredekamp & Copple, 1997, p. 129)

Inappropriate practices are those in which

> Teachers spend a great deal of time punishing unacceptable behavior, demeaning children who misbehave, repeatedly putting the same children who misbehave in time-out or some other punishment unrelated to the action. . . . Teachers do not set clear limits and do not hold children accountable to standards of acceptable behavior. The environment is chaotic, and teachers do not help children set and learn important rules of group behavior and responsibility. (Bredekamp & Copple, 1997, p. 129)

At both the preprimary and primary-grade levels, these NAEYC documents illustrate the ambiguous distinction between conventional discipline techniques and the use of punishment (Bredekamp & Copple, 1997). In fact, a growing number of early childhood professionals have become dissatisfied in recent years with the very term "discipline" (MnAEYC, 1991; Reynolds, 1996). The reason is that teachers have a hard time telling where discipline ends and punishment begins. Other educators argue that discipline is a "neutral" term and does not have to mean punishment (Marion, 1995). However, when most teachers use discipline, they tend to include acts of punishment; they mix up discipline and punishment out of anger or because they feel the child "deserves it." The very idea of "disciplining" a child suggests punishment, illustrating the easy se-mantic slide of the one into the other.

Teachers who go beyond discipline do so because of the baggage of punishment that discipline carries. These teachers reject punishment for what it is by definition: the infliction of "pain, loss, or suffering for a crime or wrongdoing."

For many years educators and psychologists have recognized the harmful effects of punishment on children (Dewey, 1900/1969; Montes-sori, 1964; Piaget, 1932/1960; Slaby, Roedell, Arezzo, & Hendrix, 1995). Some of the effects of punishment are:

- low self-esteem (feeling like a "failure").
- negative self-concept (not liking one's self).
- angry feelings (sometimes under the surface) toward others.
- a feeling of disengagement from school and the learning process.

A teacher who uses guidance knows that children learn little when the words they frequently hear are "Don't do that" or "You're naughty" or "You know better than that." When discipline includes punishment, young children have difficulty understanding how to improve their behavior (Greenberg, 1988). Instead of being shamed into "being good," they are likely to internalize the negative personal message that punishment carries (Gartrell, 1995).

Experts now recognize that through punishment children lose their trust in adults (Clewett, 1988; Slaby et al., 1995). Over time young peo-ple come to accept doing negative things and being punished for them as a natural part of life. By contrast, the increasing use of conflict manage-ment (teaching children to solve their problems with words) fosters chil-dren's faith in social processes. Conflict management and other guidance methods are being used more now because they work better than pun-ishment (Carlsson-Paige & Levin, 1992). These methods teach children how to solve problems without violence and help children to feel good about themselves, the class, and the teacher (Levin, 1994). Young chil-dren need to learn how to know better and do better. The guidance ap-proach is positive teaching, with the teacher having faith in the young child's ability to learn (Marion, 1995).

GUIDANCE: WHAT IT ISN'T

The term "discipline" remains in wide use at the elementary, middle-school, and secondary levels. Whether educators embrace the term *guidance* or at-tach a positive qualifier to "discipline," new notions about classroom man-agement can be expected that claim the use of guidance principles. With the never-ending parade of new information, it is important for us to recognize what guidance is not—so as to better understand what it is.

Five Misunderstandings about Guidance

1. Guidance Is Not Just Reacting to Problems

Many problems are caused when a teacher uses practices that are not appropriate for the age, stage, and needs of the individual child. Long group times, for instance, cause young children to become bored and restless. (They will sit in large groups more easily when they are older.) The teacher changes practices—such as reducing the number and length of group activities—to reduce the need for misbehaviors. Changes to other parts of the education program—including room layout, daily schedule, and adult-to-child ratios—also help reduce the need for misbehavior. Guidance prevents problems; it does not just react to them.

2. Guidance Does Not Mean That the Program Won't Be Educational

When activities are developmentally appropriate, *all* children succeed at them, and *all* children are learning to be successful students. The Three Rs are a part of the education program, but they are integrated into the rest of the day and made meaningful so that children want to learn. This "basic" of Progressive Education, the parent of what we now call developmentally appropriate practice, is well explained in the original and revised editions of *Developmentally Appropriate Practice in Early Childhood Programs* and both volumes of *Reaching Potentials* (Bredekamp, 1987; Bredekamp & Copple, 1997; Bredekamp & Rosegrant, 1992, 1995). When teachers use guidance, however, the Three Rs are not all there is.

The importance of guidance, according to Lilian Katz, means that the teacher makes *relationships* the first *R* (cited in Kantrowitz & Wingert, 1989). The social skills that are learned through positive relationships come first in the education program. Children need to know how to relate with others in all parts of their lives. Beginning to learn social skills in early childhood will help children in their school years and in adult life (Wittmer & Honig, 1994). (Social skills, after all, are really social studies skills and language arts skills.)

3. Guidance Is Not a "Sometimes Thing"

Some teachers think that it is natural to use "guidance" in one set of circumstances and "discipline" in another. Yet nonpunitive guidance techniques exist for all situations and, once learned, are effective (Carlsson-Paige & Levin, 1992; Reynolds, 1996). For example, a common discipline technique is the time-out chair, but the time-out chair usually embarrasses the child, seldom teaches a positive lesson, and is almost always punishment (Clewett, 1988). The teacher can cut down on the use of this punishment by reducing the need for mistaken behavior and helping children to use words to solve their problems.

If a child does lose control and needs to be removed, the teacher can stay with the child for a cooling-down time. The teacher then talks with the child about how the other child felt, helps the child find a way to help the other child feel better (make restitution), and teaches a positive alternative for next time. Guidance encompasses a full spectrum of methods, from prevention to conflict resolution to crisis intervention to long-term management strategies. Teamwork with parents and other adults is frequently part of the overall approach.

4. Guidance Is Not Permissive Discipline

Teachers who use guidance are active leaders who do not let situations get out of hand. They do not make children struggle with boundaries that may not be there (Gartrell, 1995). Guidance teachers tend to rely on guidelines—positive statements that remind children of classroom conduct—rather than rules that are usually stated in the negative, as though the adult expects the child to break them. When they intervene, teachers direct their responses to the behavior and respect the personality of the child (Ginott, 1972). They avoid embarrassment, which tends to leave lasting emotional scars. They make sure that their responses are friendly as well as firm.

The objective is to teach children to solve problems rather than to punish children for having problems they cannot solve. The outcomes of guidance—the ability to get along with others, solve problems using words, express strong feelings in acceptable ways—are the goals for citizens of a democratic society. For this reason, guidance has a meaning that goes beyond traditional discipline. Guidance is not just keeping children in line; it is actively teaching them skills they will need for their entire lives (Wittmer & Honig, 1994).

5. Guidance Is Not Reducible to a Commercial Program

The guidance tradition is part of the child-sensitive educational practice of the last two decades. Guidance is part of the movement toward developmentally appropriate and culturally responsive education. Teachers who use guidance rely on a teaching team (adults in the classroom working together) and positive parent-teacher relations. Guidance involves more than a workshop or a program on paper; it requires reflective commitment by the teacher, teamwork by the staff, and cooperation with families and the community.

SIX KEY GUIDANCE PRACTICES

Teachers who use guidance have classrooms that are encouraging places to be in. In the words of one teacher, when guidance is present, children want to come to school even when they are sick. Both children and adults feel welcome in guidance classrooms. An informed observer who visits such a classroom quickly sees that "guidance is practiced here." Six key guidance practices follow. When they are evident in a classroom, the teacher is using guidance.

1. The Teacher Realizes That Social Skills Are Complicated and Take into Adulthood to Fully Learn

In the process of learning social skills, children—like all of us—make mistakes. That's why behaviors traditionally considered to be "misbehaviors" are regarded as "mistaken behaviors" (Gartrell, 1987a, 1987b, 1995). The teacher believes in the positive potential of each child. He recognizes that mistaken behaviors are caused by inexperience in social situations, the influence of others on the child, or by deep, unmet physical or emotional needs. Understanding why children show mistaken behavior permits the teacher to teach social skills with a minimum of moral judgment about the child. He takes the attitude that "we all make mistakes; we just need to learn from them."

The teacher shows this understanding even when the children demonstrate "strong-needs" (serious) mistaken behavior (Gartrell, 1987b, 1995). Such children are sometimes regarded as "bad" children, but the teacher using guidance knows that they are children with bad problems that they cannot solve on their own. In working with strong-needs mistaken behavior, the teacher takes a comprehensive approach. He seeks to understand the problem, modifies the child's program to reduce crises, intervenes consistently but nonpunitively, builds the relationship with the child, involves the parents, teams with staff and other professionals, and develops, implements, and monitors a long-term plan.

2. The Teacher Reduces the Need for Mistaken Behavior

One major cause of mistaken behavior is a poor match between the child and the educational program (the program expects either too much or too little from the child). The teacher improves the match by using teaching practices that are developmentally appropriate and culturally sensitive (Bredekamp, 1987; Bredekamp & Copple, 1997). She reduces wait times by offering many activities in learning centers and small groups. She gives children choices so they can work at their own levels in activities. To avoid problems, she anticipates when particular children will need support and encouragement. She changes activities, adjusts the schedule, and modifies the room arrangement as circumstances warrant. She uses adults in the classroom to increase individual attention and expand opportunities for positive adult-child attachments. When children's development, learning styles, and family backgrounds become the main priorities of a program, children become positively involved and feel less need to show mistaken behavior.

3. The Teacher Practices Positive Teacher-Child Relations

The teacher works to accept each child as a welcome member of the class (Warren, 1977). To prevent embarrassment and unnecessary competition, the teacher avoids singling out children either for criticism or praise. Instead, she uses private feedback with the individual and group-focused encouragement with the class (Hitz & Driscoll, 1988).

Even if children are preschoolers, the teacher holds class meetings both for regular business and for problems that arise (Brewer, 1992). The teacher relies more on guidelines—positive statements of expected behaviors—than on rules with negative wording and implied threats. She models and teaches cooperation and empathy-building skills. She models and teaches acceptance of children who might be singled out negatively for physical, cultural, or behavioral reasons. She teaches that differing human qualities and circumstances are natural, to be appreciated and learned from. She understands that children who feel accepted in the classroom have less need to show mistaken behavior.

4. The Teacher Uses Intervention Methods That Are Solution Oriented

The teacher creates an environment in which problems can be solved peaceably (Levin, 1994). He intervenes by modeling and teaching conflict management—initially using high-level mediation and continually encouraging the children to negotiate for themselves. He avoids public embarrassment and rarely uses removal (redirection and cooling-down times) or physical restraint, and then only as methods of last resort. After intervention, the teacher assists the child with regaining composure, understanding the other's feelings, learning more acceptable behaviors, and making amends and reconciling with the other child or group.

The teacher recognizes that, at times, he too shows human frailties. The teacher works at monitoring and managing his own feelings. The teacher learns even as he teaches. As a developing professional, the teacher models the effort to learn from mistakes.

5. The Teacher Builds Partnerships with Parents

The teacher recognizes that mistaken behavior occurs less often when parents and teachers work together. The teacher also recognizes that being a parent is a difficult job and that many parents, for personal and cultural reasons, feel uncomfortable meeting with educators (Gestwicki, 2004). The teacher starts building partnerships at the beginning of the year. Through positive notes home, phone calls, visits, meetings, and conferences, she builds relationships. It is her job to build partnerships even with hard-to-reach parents. When the invitations are sincere, many parents gradually do become involved.

6. The Teacher Uses Teamwork with Adults

The teacher recognizes that it is a myth that she can handle all situations alone. She creates a teaching team of fellow staff and volunteers (especially parents) who work together in the classroom. She understands that children gain trust in their world when they see adults of differing backgrounds working together. When there is serious mistaken behavior, the teacher meets with parents and other adults to develop and use a coordinated plan. Through coordinated assistance, children can be helped to overcome serious problems and build self-esteem and social skills. The teacher knows that effective communication among adults builds a bridge between school and community. Through working together, teachers accomplish what they cannot do alone.

In summary, guidance goes beyond the traditional goal of classroom discipline: enforcing children's compliance to the teacher's will. On a day-to-day basis in the classroom, guidance teaches children the life skills they need as citizens of a democracy. Teachers encourage children to take pride in their developing personalities and cultural identities. Guidance teaches children to view differing human qualities as sources of affirmation and learning.

Guidance involves creating a successful learning environment for each child. The teacher plans and implements an educational program that is developmentally appropriate and culturally responsive. She or he serves as leader of a classroom community and helps all children to find a place and to learn. The teacher uses nonpunitive intervention techniques, in firm but friendly ways, to establish guidelines and guide children's behavior. She or he uses conflict resolution as a regular and important tool.

The guidance approach involves teamwork on the part of adults, especially in the face of serious mistaken behavior. Guidance links together teacher, parent, and child on a single team. Success in the use of guidance is measured not in test scores or "obedient" classes but in positive attitudes in the classroom community toward living and learning.

End Note: *This chapter first appeared in the September 1997 issue of* Young Children. *It is referenced as follows: Gartrell, D. J. (1997). Beyond discipline to guidance.* Young Children *52(6), 34–42.*

REFERENCES

Bredekamp, S. (Ed.). (1987). *Developmentally appropriate practice in early childhood programs serving children from birth through age 8* (Exp. ed.). Washington, DC: NAEYC.

Bredekamp, S., & Copple, C. (Eds.). (1997). *Developmentally appropriate practice in early childhood programs* (Rev. ed.). Washington, DC: NAEYC.

Bredekamp, S., & Rosegrant, T. (Eds.). (1992). *Reaching potentials: Appropriate curriculum and assessment for young children* (Vol. 1). Washington, DC: NAEYC.

Bredekamp, S., & Rosegrant, T. (Eds.). (1995). *Reaching potentials: Transforming early childhood curriculum and assessment* (Vol. 2). Washington, DC: NAEYC.

Brewer, J. A. (1992). Where does it all begin? Teaching the principles of democracy in the early years. *Young Children 47*(3), 51–53.

Carlsson-Paige, N., & Levin, D. E. (1992). Making peace in violent times: A constructivist approach to conflict resolution. *Young Children 48* (1), 4–13.*

Clewett, A. S. (1988). Guidance and discipline: Teaching young children appropriate behavior. *Young Children 43*(4), 22–36.*

Curwin, R. L., & Mendler, A. N. (1988). *Discipline with dignity.* Alexandria, VA: Association for Supervision and Curriculum Development.

Dewey, J. (1969). *The school and society.* Chicago: University of Chicago Press. (Original work published 1900)

Dreikurs, R. (1968). *Psychology in the classroom.* New York: Harper & Row.

Gartrell, D. J. (1987a). Assertive discipline: Unhealthy for children and other living things. *Young Children 42*(2), 10–11.

Gartrell, D. J. (1987b). Punishment or guidance. *Young Children 42*(3), 55–61.

Gartrell, D. J. (1995). Misbehavior or mistaken behavior? *Young Children 50*(5), 27–34.

Gestwicki, C. (2004). Home, school and community relations (5th ed.). Clifton Park, NY: Delmar Learning.

Ginott, H. (1972). *Teacher and child.* New York: Avon.

Greenberg, P. (1988). Avoiding "me against you" discipline. *Young Children 43*(1), 24–25.*

Hitz, R. (1988). Viewpoint. Assertive discipline: A response to Lee Canter. *Young Children 43*(2), 25–26.

Hitz, R., & Driscoll, A. (1988). Praise or encouragement? New insights into praise: Implications for early childhood teachers. *Young Children 43*(4), 6–13.

Hymes, J. L. (1949). *Discipline.* New York: Bureau of Publications, Columbia University.

Hymes, J. L. (1953). *Effective home-school relations.* Englewood Cliffs, NJ: Prentice Hall.

Hymes, J. L. (1955). *Behavior and misbehavior.* Englewood Cliffs, NJ: Prentice Hall.

Janke, A. J., & Penshorn Peterson, J. (1995). *Peacemaker's A,B,Cs for young children.* S. Marine on St. Croix, MN: Growing Communities for Peace.*

Kamii, C. (1984). Autonomy: The aim of education envisioned by Piaget. *Phi Delta Kappan 65*(6), 410–415.

Kantrowitz, B., & Wingert, P. (1989, July 17). How kids learn. *Newsweek,* 50–56.

Levin, D. E. (1994). *Teaching young children in violent times.* Cambridge, MA: Educators for Social Responsibility.

Lilley, I. M., (Ed.). (1967). *Friedrich Froebel: A selection from his writings.* London: Cambridge University Press.

Marion, M. (1995). *Guidance of young children* (5th ed.). Columbus, OH: Merrill.

Minnesota Association for the Education of Young Children (MnAEYC). (1991). *Developmentally appropriate guidance of children birth to eight.* (Rev. ed.). St. Paul: Author.

Montessori, M. (1964). *The Montessori method.* New York: Schocken.

Osborn, D. K. (1980). *Early childhood education in historical perspective.* Athens, GA: Education Associates.

Piaget, J. (1960). *The moral judgment of the child.* Glencoe, IL: Free Press. (Original work published 1932)

Read, K. H. [1950] (1993). *Early childhood programs: Human relations and learning* (9th ed.). Fort Worth, TX: Harcourt Brace.

Reynolds, E. (1996). *Guiding young children: A child-centered approach* (2nd ed.). Mountain View, CA: Mayfield.

Slaby, R. G., Roedell, W. C., Arezzo, D., & Hendrix, K. (1995). *Early violence prevention: Tools for teachers of young children.* Washington, DC: NAEYC.

Standing, E. M. (1962). *Maria Montessori: Her life and work.* New York: New American Library.

Stone, J. G. (1978). *A guide to discipline* (Rev. ed.). Washington, DC: NAEYC.

Warren, R. M. (1977). *Caring: Supporting children's growth.* Washington, DC: NAEYC.

Wichert, S. (1989). *Keeping the peace: Practicing cooperation and conflict resolution with preschoolers.* Philadelphia: New Society.*

Wittmer, D. S., & Honig, A. S. (1994). Encouraging positive social development in young children. *Young Children 49*(5), 61–75.*

*Recommended reading.

FOR FURTHER READING

Greenberg, P. (1990). Ideas that work with young children. Why not academic preschool? (Pt. 1). *Young Children 45*(2), 70–80.

Greenberg, P. (1992). Why not academic preschool? (Pt. 2). Autocracy or democracy in the classroom? *Young Children 47*(3), 54–64.

Greenberg, P. (1992). Ideas that work with young children. How to institute some simple democratic practices pertaining to respect, rights, roots, and responsibilities in any classroom (without losing your leadership position). *Young Children 47*(5), 10–17.

Hendrick, J. (1992). Where does it all begin? Teaching the principles of democracy in the early years. *Young Children 47*(3), 51–64.

The Guidance Premise: Family-Teacher Partnerships

QUICK TAKE

If guidance is to have any power at all, it must be grounded in family-teacher partnerships. Sometimes writers think that when it comes to behavior in the classroom, the teacher does it all; they may include material about connecting with parents, but usually as an afterthought. In my textbook, *A Guidance Approach for the Encouraging Classroom* (3rd ed.) (2003), I concluded each chapter with a section on the family, . . . so at least there was an afterthought for each chapter. The format of this book did not allow for a similar approach, but now, after basic concepts of guidance have been introduced, the placement seems right for a chapter about building partnerships with families.*

*The significant adults in a child's life are sometimes other than parents. I use the term *family* when possible to acknowledge this fact. Further, I ask that readers consider my use of the term *parent* to include those very special adult caregivers, parents in soul and spirit if not in the literal definition of the term.

Why at this point in the book? If in January a child has an accident on the playground and breaks an arm, teachers want to be contacting a parent they have known since the beginning of the year—not a parent they have only briefly met. This chapter appears here, and not at the end of the book, to remind teachers that partnerships with families start right away when a child and family first begin the program, and not only when something serious happens.

Besides its focus on families, Chapter 4 is different from the preceding chapters in another way. It is not adapted from a single publication. Instead, Parts One, Two, and Three of the chapter come from my book *What the Kids Said Today: Using Classroom Conversations to Become a Better Teacher* (2000),* while Part Four comes from my textbook, *A Guidance Approach for the Encouraging Classroom* (3rd ed.) 2003. Rather than develop the theme linearly, each part talks to the theme, family-teacher partnerships, from different perspectives. Only the last part directly addresses guidance issues; still my hope is that by the end of the chapter readers will see how the four parts blend in this discussion of "the guidance premise."

PART ONE: THE FAMILY AND THE SCHOOL

In an often-quoted passage of early childhood literature, Polly Greenberg (1989) said:

> Children whose parents expect them to cooperate and to do their best at school, and who are proud when they do, tend to have better self-discipline. [These children] are striving to achieve family approval; to do this they must earn the teacher's approval. Encouraging a high degree of family enthusiasm for their children's public schools and child care centers is one of the best ways in which teachers can . . . build children's self-esteem and reduce discipline problems. (pp. 61–62)

---

*Parts One, Two, and Three also use several anecdotes to illustrate ideas—the approach used throughout *What the Kids Said Today* (Gartrell, 2000).

An absolutely sparkling concept, but the complication is that due to their own schooling experiences, some parents lack faith in the institutions they send their children to. They are uncomfortable even talking with teachers. (A parent I know has to fight the urge to wretch whenever he enters a school building—this after many years out of school.) While not all parents feel this way, many do. *Part One of the chapter* suggests why a rift historically has existed between schools and too many parents, and what teachers can do about it.

Giving Them Over to the School

Over the years a mistaken practice in education has been to consider the child in the classroom separate from the child in the family. Teachers make this error, often without thinking about it, when they consider life in the classroom as a partial replacement for the life of the child in the home. Examples of the attitude can be seen in such statements as, "You are a big child at school now and not a baby at home anymore." Or, "You may act this way at home, but you do not act this way here at school." These statements indicate the teacher is giving inflated importance to the socializing influence of the school and diminishing the importance of the family.

This error in judgment by the teacher undermines the child's natural identification with the family, as well as personal identity as a family member. It tends to split school influence from family influence in the child's mind, putting the child in the difficult position of having to choose between competing cultures. For children whose family backgrounds and values are similar to the teacher's, this "marginal status" (being caught between two cultures) is less extreme, but is still real. With children whose home culture is especially different from the school's—a different language is spoken, for instance—the child's marginal status is extreme indeed.

This unfortunate attitude—that the school "takes over" for the home as socializing institution—has its roots in our history and is a remnant of the *melting pot* function of American schools. From the end of the Civil War to World War II, the population of the United States was greatly increased by immigrants, many who spoke little English and knew little of American life. For political as well as educational reasons, schools were charged with "Americanizing the aliens" (an actual phrase from a government publication—Locke, 1919). For much of the 20th century educators, especially in public schools, did little to change this view and many regarded parents not as partners, but as "clients"—in the officious sense of the term (Greenberg, 1989).

As a result of the melting pot theory, many immigrant parents, as well as parents from native minority groups, felt they were "giving their children over to the school." In other words upon entrance to school, parents gave up significant rights in relation to raising their children.

For the Good of the Child

In contrast to this (hopefully fading) melting pot ideology, some teachers always have seen the importance of home and school working together. They pride themselves on building and maintaining close ties with parents. The complaint of "too much institutional control over children's lives" is certainly not the fault of early childhood programs, which usually are not required and are there to serve families' needs.

In fact, the relative success of early childhood teachers at forging home-school partnerships is undoubtedly due to the recognition of teachers that the family is so important to young children. Although some critics might argue differently, early childhood systems such as Head Start provide a clear American model for how the "home versus school" issue can be made obsolete. The early childhood model points instead to how the child's growing sense of community can include both home and school.

The position here is not that preschool programs have solved the riddle of how to involve parents in the education of their children, but that public schools have not. Rather, early childhood programs have contributed approaches to working with parents that are based *less* on the power of the school as socializing institution versus the family, and more on a model of partnership on behalf of the child (Workman & Gage, 1997).

In making connections with families, teachers face the uncertainties that come with cultural differences. Whether due to ethnic, racial, religious, or lifestyle factors, these differences can and sometimes do make building teacher-family relationships difficult. The teacher's ability to become understanding in such situations, to be open to the experience of the family, is essential. We conclude this part with an anecdote, set in an elementary school. In the anecdote Mavis, an experienced kindergarten teacher, recalls her experience with a family that, as a result of their religious beliefs, other teachers found difficult. Read how Mavis stays with this family, bringing us back around to Greenberg's opening quote.

A necdote

In my first year, a veteran teacher told me to "watch out" for a certain family. Their younger child was to be in my kindergarten class. The family was Jehovah's Witnesses. As part of their faith, the family taught their children not to salute the flag or celebrate birthdays and holidays. This teacher told me that in the previous year the parents had become irate when they were not told of a Halloween party in the classroom of the older child, even though their child had not participated. The teacher then tried to let the family know of upcoming events, but she felt they remained distant and uncooperative. There were instances when the older child, now a third grader, had been made fun of by classmates. The parents reported these incidents, but the teacher apparently told the family there was not much she could do.

I remembered going to school when I was in fourth grade with a child of this faith. I remembered thinking how hard it must be for him to be left out of important school events. I took this teacher's comments as a personal challenge, and decided to work hard to get along with this family. It was my practice to send home notes of introduction to each family before school began and then continue with "happy-grams" home on a rotating basis for each member of my class. I made sure this child went home with at least one complimentary note every week. This was not a hard task. I enjoyed the child's pluckiness. (I read each note to her just to make sure it would get delivered.) I called the home a few times as well, but always got an answering machine. I left messages that I hoped the parents would find friendly.

Other teachers told me not to expect this family to attend the fall parent conference, but the mother did come. I was pleased to see her, and she seemed rather surprised at my reaction. I decided to let her bring up the religion issue. My job was to let her know how well her daughter was doing in my class. Well, she did bring it up. I told her I was interested to hear about her faith (because I was). She told me about the flag salute, and I said not to worry—we wouldn't be doing the flag salute until close to the end of the year because I didn't think the children could understand it. She smiled at this.

About birthdays, I told her what I told all the parents: I preferred that the children had parties at home, but we let the children wear a "birthday crown" for the day if that was okay with the parents. She said no crown for Wilma, but otherwise she liked what I did. About holiday activities, I asked her what she would like me to do, and we had quite a conversation about that. I was very surprised when she said Wilma could stay in the classroom if I could figure out a way to have her fit in without participating. That year, I kind of downplayed the holidays, explaining to the parents who asked that not all of the children in the class celebrate all holidays. I did more with the ideas behind the holidays—for instance, what we should be thankful for—rather than do pageants and crafts—a practice I still follow today.

What I am still the proudest about with this family had to do with the flag salute. Before we started doing the flag salute in April, I had three parents come in to discuss with the class what saluting the flag meant to them. One was Wilma's mom, and she did a fine job of explaining why Wilma would stand up (out of respect for the class), but wouldn't be doing the rest. (I had previously told the other two parents what Wilma's mom would say and they were okay with this—one commented there are different ways to be an American.) That whole year, I never did remember any of the children making fun of Wilma—they liked her, just as I did.

As Mavis showed through her anecdote, teachers can regard "nonmainstream" cultural differences not as roadblocks, but as sources of learning and mutual appreciation. This section on the relation of the family to the school reminds us that teachers can make the family ties, so necessary for children, a natural and accepted part of the educational program. As they mature, there will be time enough for children to separate from the family—for the purposes of education, work, starting families of their own, and other life circumstances. While they are young, the connection that children feel to their families should be celebrated in the classroom so that each child feels full and healthy membership with the classroom community as well as with a family at home. As Greenberg (1989) suggested, children secure in their relationships with family *and* teachers have little need to act out against the world.

PART TWO: SUPPORTING CHILDREN'S TIES TO THEIR FAMILIES

In a partnership model, the teacher supports each child's ties to the family, as an important foundation on which to build a life. The teacher assists children to extend their home lives into the classroom and augments, rather than replaces, children's all-important family experiences.

The reason is clear, family life is never far from the mind of the young child. Family life is the experience that children know best. If children feel that their thoughts about family are natural and completely acceptable in the classroom, they will extend their sense of community to include both home and school. Children will be able to see themselves as accepted and productive members of each group. The contrasting experience, feeling that the teacher rejects one's family, causes children to feel rejected as well. Adrift in the classroom, these children feel alienated from the complex expectations and relationships of classroom life (Galinksy, 1988). They feel stress and react against their feelings of rejection. Though it never should be, strong-needs mistaken behavior *caused within the classroom* results.

Part Two explores how a teacher can assist children to feel part of the encouraging classroom, by showing them their families have a place as well.

Two Basic Tools

One established tool for learning about children and ties to their families is **observation**. Teachers often say that they learn so much from observing children in the classroom. What they do with this information has always interested me. If the knowledge helps the teacher to understand and accept child and family, then observation is an important skill indeed. In my experience teachers who are open enough to observe children, carefully and nonjudgmentally, tend to be understanding of, and fundamentally helpful to, children—and their families.

An important "arena" for observing children, of course, is their dramatic play—both alone with miniature figures (including diverse dolls of course) and together with other children. At an early age children already have begun learning about the roles and activities of adults. They learn even more as they act out family situations in their play. The social give-and-take by a child with a miniature figure or with other children indicates so clearly the importance of family in children's lives. Family study might well be the "major" of most children in early childhood programs:

Anecdote

During my observation of play in a kindergarten class, I was able to see three children working hard at playing house. The children are Rachel, Jeremiah (Mia), and Sarah. Rachel is preparing a meal in the kitchen. She is wearing an apron and cooking on the stove with a frying pan. "Good morning, Honey," said Rachel as she smiled at Mia and continued to cook.

"Good morning to you, Cupcake," said Mia. As he walked up to Sarah, Mia asked, "How is our big girl doing today?"

"Fine, Daddy," said Sarah as she held her baby doll.

"Breakfast is ready, have Sarah sit down and it is time to eat," said Rachel. Rachel made a motion to have them sit at the table and they did. I noticed that Sarah dropped her baby doll and started to prefer drinking from a glass instead of the sipper cup that was on the table. Both Mia and Sarah were sitting at the kitchen table being served by Mom. Then they all said a prayer and began to eat.

"I'm filled," said Mia, "I am late for work." Mia grabbed a hard hat out of the toy box and he gave Rachel a kiss good-bye (which was promptly wiped off!). When Mia was gone, Rachel started to clear the table, putting the dishes in the sink. Sarah walked over to the baby doll she had dropped and picked it up. She began holding the doll in her arms and wanted mommy (Rachel) to play with her.

"I have to finish the dishes before I can go out and play," said Rachel.

"I want to play with you now," demanded Sarah.

"Barney is on now, go and watch him," said Rachel. Rachel continued to wash the dishes and Sarah went over to the TV and watched Barney. Mia also headed into the kitchen area; he had been just wandering around and fixing things in the playroom.

"Honey, I'm home," said Mia.

"You're home early," said Rachel. "Go back to work, I'm not done yet."

"I'm bored. I'm going to play with something different now," said Mia. He left the area and soon Rachel and Sarah did, too.

This anecdote is notable for the realistic detail—and the particular customs—these children brought to their family situation. So much language, social, personal, and even physical development comes from dramatic play like this. The observation is also notable because Myra, the student teacher who observed it, informed me that none of the three children came from a traditional two-parent family! The prevalence of the image of the traditional family, even for young children, often permeates their play. Because children depend so completely on their families, an important lesson for them to learn is that families can take many shapes and forms—by looking at the actual families represented by the class. If teachers perpetuate the image of the traditional family, some children in virtually any class are going to feel that their family doesn't fit, isn't OK.

Contact Talks

A teacher learns from observations either as an onlooker outside of a situation or as a "participant observer" engaging with children during their activities. Informal conversations are fundamental to learning about children's connections to their families (Howard, Shaughnessy, Sanger, & Hux, 1998). These conversations can occur at any time, but often happen during play situations, informal activities, and at meal or snack times. The term I give to the *second tool* for supporting children in the classroom is **contact talk. Contact talks** are conversations that an adult has with children in order to understand them better. In contact talks, the adult makes a conscious decision to have the conversation, listens and attempts to follow the child's lead, and shares a quality moment with the child (rather than use the conversation to "teach, preach, or screech"—smile).

Teachers sometimes feel they don't have time for contact talks, but in reality the talks happen all of the time and don't have to be lengthy at all. When they realize that they often have contact talks, teachers notice three characteristics that make them worthwhile:

First, with the adult's undivided attention, children develop their thoughts, use rich language, share their feelings, and register the adult's responses. These qualities make contact talks sources of significant learning for the child (Kratcoski & Katz,1998).

Second, after a contact talk, the adult will feel she or he is a bit more attached with the child—mutual acceptance and trust have increased a bit.

Third, through contact talks, teachers learn about the joys and concerns of children—and see the particular ways that a child's world is bound up in the family.

> While sitting at the lunch table during Head Start, we were talking about families. One child chimed,"I have a sister." Several other children began talking about their siblings as well.
>
> One little boy says,"I have a half sister."
>
> I replied,"You have a half sister, Damon?"
>
> He looked at me nodding and said, "Yep, and when she grows up, she's gonna be a whole sister." Damon and I looked at each other and smiled.

Neddie, the teacher, mentioned that she did not know if Damon had thought this idea up himself or if it was "a happy family joke." Neddie did see, though, that Damon was pleased about his half sister, and she affirmed his feeling by reflecting his comment back to him and sharing a smile. When a teacher acknowledges the thoughts and feelings of a child (called "reflective listening," "active listening," or "acknowledgment"), she actively supports the child's confidence and competence at communication—even with only a brief comment and a smile.

Observing and Talking When Children Feel Hurt

Through self-expression in dramatic play, art, or conversation, children celebrate happy moments in family life, but also attempt to understand and grieve other moments that are not so happy (Curry & Arnaud, 1995). Teachers witness the sadder aspects of child expression as well, for it is a mistake to conclude that childhood is always a happy time and that children are oblivious to difficulty. The information gained from observation when children feel pain allows the teacher to be effectively supportive.

OBSERVATION

Three preschool children were building a structure with blocks and colorful, plastic bricks. It was really fancy and had a road leading up to it and even a parking lot. I noticed that some of the play cars were police cars, and I asked Jackson what they were building. He said, "The law 'forcement compex." A few minutes later Jackson took his miniature figure out of a car and approached another child holding a second figure. "Excuse me, sir," he said, "Can you tell me where the Juv'nile Center is?"

REFLECTION

I knew from talking with Jackson's Mom that morning that his brother had gone into the Juvenile Detention Center the day before. His Mom hadn't taken Jackson, but had told him they could visit his brother on the weekend. Jackson later talked with me about his brother, and I showed him on the calendar how many days until Saturday and Sunday and helped him count the days on his fingers. He seemed relieved to know that the weekend was coming in three days.

Whatever problems family members encounter, children may express those situations in their play. Teachers, like Abby in the anecdote, assist children to make sense of life when they observe carefully, and are able to communicate with parents to fully understand the meaning of the child's play. Observation in itself does not resolve children's problems. Still, in an encouraging classroom, when teachers observe and understand how family events affect a child at play, they are in a position to take steps—like responding to other behaviors of the child and offering comfort through contact talks—that can help.

Moving Between Child and Parent

As soon as a child joins the program, teachers in the encouraging classroom work to build positive relations with families. The teacher who has developed partnerships can provide support sensitively and effectively when the child is in need. In the next anecdote, notice how "seamlessly" Connie, the teacher, goes from child to mother to child again in order to figure out a problem the child has and find a solution.

We have visitors in the Head Start center today, a psychologist and a Health Services nurse. We hear the children enter the classroom and greet us after a long weekend at home.

Harris: "Teacher, I hate you."

Me: "Can you tell me about why you hate me?"

Harris: "No." Harris walks away with head down.

I call Mom to find out what she knows. I find out that Harris's Dad had been visiting from Alaska and is leaving today while Harris is at the Center. Mom and I agree that he is probably upset about his Dad leaving and Harris having to be at class. I ask Mom how she feels about Harris missing Center. She said she thought it best he not miss out on Center. I gave her the option of rethinking. She decides to drive in and pick up her child, who is standing, still in coat and boots.

Me: "I talked to Mom and she has decided that this is a special day for you, she will come and pick you up."

Harris: "Can I go eat and play?"

Me: "How about you get your coat and boots off, wash your hands, eat breakfast, brush your teeth, and if there is time, play."

Harris: "Connie, I love you."

The words, "I hate you," are so powerful that they frequently make teachers feel angry, and maybe even hateful too. Connie did not listen to the literal meaning of the words, but heard instead something like this: "Connie, 'I am dying here!' My Dad is leaving. I don't want to be at Center today, and it's maybe your fault that I am, and I don't know how to ask for help, but I need it." Connie took what Harris said seriously, but not personally. She was able to use that unique skill of caring adults: "Don't listen to what I say, listen to what I mean."

Connie's responsiveness not only prompted her to listen openly, but to call the parent whom she knew and figure out a way to get Harris help. The partnership that Connie had with the family allowed her to de-escalate mistaken behavior that could well have gotten worse. Connie's anecdote illustrates well the importance of family-teacher partnerships for the power of guidance. Harris and his mother both found reason to value their relationships with this teacher.

PART THREE: BUILDING PARTNERSHIPS

In the encouraging classroom teachers build partnerships with parents in order to bridge differences between home and school and to empower the home-school connection. These teachers recognize that how they respond to the child's family affects the behavior of the child at school. *Part Three* looks at four kinds of parent-teacher communication used in early childhood education: telephone contacts, conferences, home visits, and classroom contacts with volunteers in the classroom. My intent is to share anecdotes about successful contacts in these four areas for readers to think about in relation to their own professional priorities.

Phone Calls

A clear example of the effective use of the phone call was provided in the last anecdote, when Connie called Harris's Mom to figure out a problem. Connie used the telephone to *maintain* positive teacher-parent-child relations. Another use of the phone is at the beginning of the school year to build positive relations. Here is a profile of how Pat, a longtime kindergarten teacher in northern Minnesota, builds relations through phone calls:

> Pat takes a four-step approach to make connections with parents and children at the beginning of the year. A week or two before school starts Pat sends a note to each child on Garfield stationery saying how happy she is that he or she is in her class. She tells the child to watch for the Garfield the Cat picture outside of her room. She also writes to the parents, introducing herself and giving some guidelines for her classroom to help the year start off right. In the letter to the parents, she includes both her school and home phone numbers. [Giving out a home phone number is something not every teacher is comfortable with. Pat says in her 30 plus years, she has never had a parent abuse this practice.] A day or two before start-up, Pat calls every child. She tells them again she is happy to be their teacher and reassures them that they will have a great time in her class.
>
> Pat says the single most productive step she takes in terms of building relations each year is to call each family on the evening of the first day of school. She talks with the parents about any

problems with bus rides, during the day, etc., and gives the child any needed first night reassurance. Once when a child had a particularly difficult first day, Pat asked the parent if there were a jar of peanut butter in the house that the child could bring in next day, because "we could really use that peanut butter to put on crackers for a snack." The next morning the child proudly brought in the peanut butter, and Pat expressed her appreciation—and relief when the kid had a much better day.

Pat says on that first night she would much rather drink a beverage of her choice and hit the sack early. When she notes the responsiveness of parents to her program over the next few weeks, Pat knows why she makes these calls each year.

Phone calls are helpful for many types of communication between teacher and parent. The exception is discussion of a serious problem. If it's serious, the talk should be face-to-face. When both teacher and parent have access to phones, and speak a common language, the value of phone calls to forge and maintain parent-teacher partnerships is pretty much granted. But not all teachers have telephones in their classrooms, and not all parents have phones in their homes, or speak the teacher's language. When phone calls are not an option, teachers turn to notes home and home visits, depending on the circumstances. (Increasingly, with some families in almost every classroom e-mail correspondence is also becoming an option, with its own advantages and caveats [Gartrell, 2003].)

Home Visits

Home visits by early childhood teachers are not new. In the last century, Froebel's kindergartens in Germany and later in the United States included home visits. During the first half of the 20th century both federal and state governments encouraged home visits by kindergarten teachers as a way to reach immigrant families.

Progressive early childhood programs, and especially Head Start, always have included home visits as a strategy to reach the family. Head Start home visitors work with both the family and child and are known for being part social worker and part early childhood teacher—one tough job. In this day and age home visitors usually have connections to classrooms that the children also attend. Home visits by teachers help them to learn about family dynamics and children's response styles in ways they cannot within the confines of the classroom alone (Johnston & Mermin, 1994). In the following anecdote, Julie, a student teacher in a Head Start program, accompanied the teacher to Maya's home. Note the understanding that Julie gains about Maya from the experience.

During a home visit to Maya's home we did several things. While the teacher talked with Maya's Mom about some recipes and getting fuel assistance, Maya and I made play dough. Maya mixed it all herself, then began playing with it. She put her ring in the dough, then used another piece to make a treasure map. When Mom and the teacher got done, she asked Mom to use the map and try to find the ring. She did this over and over while we were there. Every time, she would giggle and laugh, then start over after the ring had been found. After this, Mom read Maya a book we had brought; we had a snack, and said good-bye.

REFLECTION

Maya has never laughed at school the way she did at home. I think this is because she is more comfortable at home. I saw a side of her that I had not previously seen. With the playdough, her attention span was longer than any of the adults [smile]. She would have continued to hide the ring all day if the home visit had not come to an end.

Diane, an experienced Head Start teacher, confirmed for me Julie's experience in the anecdote, that a teacher can learn so much about a child from making home visits. Before she made home visits, Diane encountered a few children each year who were hard for her to understand and work with, sometimes all year. She said that after she began making home visits, she has not had this problem. She understands the children more fully, and what ever they learned about her, they seemed to be more accepting of her leadership in the classroom. Healthy, mutual attachments with the children and their families were easier to make and keep.

Parent-Teacher-Child Conferences

Conferences offer the teacher a unique opportunity for information about the family that adds to understanding and teaching effectiveness. When done in a positive, nonthreatening manner, conferences also increase parent interest and involvement in their child's education. An important trend in conferencing at all levels is to include the learner along with the parents (Taylor, 1999). Teachers' first reactions to this prospect are guarded; they find they have to approach both material and the communication process differently with the learner there. A common reflection after teachers get used to this format is that under most circumstances, they wouldn't have conferences any other way. Often the young child will sit in for part of the conference, then be free to play in the classroom if the discussion gets too involved.

The following write-up by a student teacher, Marta, is a primer on the purpose and the conduct of parent-teacher-child conferences. Marta's role in some of the conferences was to read a book or do a puzzle with the children while their parents continued to talk with the teacher.

OBSERVATION

As a student teacher I was invited to sit in on the spring conferences for my second grade class. When my cooperating teacher first asked me this, I was surprised because I had not taught enough of the class to really have a valuable insight into the children's performance. I realized later that it was a great learning experience for me, more than my benefiting the parent and child.

Roberta had prepared an individual folder for each of the children. It contained samples of their work since the last conference as well as some of their previous work so she could show each parent and child their improvements. She also included some checklists and other assessment material that went along with the school's curriculum. She included in the folders a sheet so she could record parents' comments and refer back to them in the future.

At the beginning of each conference Roberta would greet the parents and child and invite them to take seats next to her. She would tell the parents how much she enjoyed having their child in her class. She had something positive to say about each child. Roberta would then move on to showing the parents their children's work, asking the children to explain their pictures, journal entries, etc. With the children's help she would point out improvements and also showed the parents how they could help their children at home. She would always have inexpensive resources such as library books and "counting beans" in a jar and show the parents how to play the Bean Game.

If a child were in a special program, she would also go over these assessments and tell the parents how they were doing in the Title One program. Roberta ended each conference by going over her notes with the parents, and pointing out what more she and the parents could do to help the child continue to make progress. She always seemed to end the conferences on a positive note.

During one conference, Roberta was speaking with a father of one of the girls in the class who was receiving extra assistance through Title One. Cheyenne (the daughter) and I had gone over to the puzzles, but I couldn't help but hear the rest of the conference because the father was really upset. He was Native American and had a very bad experience when he was in school in the special education program. He was adamant that he did not want his daughter in the Title program. [The Mother had placed her in the program.] I was uncomfortable sitting there, but the teacher stayed very calm.

Roberta acknowledged the pain he felt and expressed understanding. Then she explained how the Title program works today. The children are not removed from the class, they are not treated like outcasts, and the other children treat them no differently. She showed the parent how much his daughter had improved and told him if he would be more comfortable, she would decrease his daughter's aid because she had come so far. Roberta asked him if he had any suggestions for her about how she could better help his daughter. She took notes and they agreed on a plan for Cheyenne. When he left he was happy with how the conference had gone. I don't think Cheyenne had caught the more serious parts of the conference, and her smile at the end when I said good-bye told me that she was happy about it too.

REFLECTION

I thought that Roberta did a wonderful job with the conferences. She started every conference on a positive note. When she went over the child's work, she inquired about any issues the parents may wish to discuss. When the teacher was dealing with the father who was upset, if she had invited him to sit across from her desk, he may have felt intimidated, which probably would have made him more on edge. When the teacher sat next to him, I think he felt more comfortable. In addition, she used reflective listening with him, responding to his complaint of his own problems with the special education program. Roberta used compliment sandwiches; too, mentioning that while Cheyenne still needed Title aid, she was making progress and improvements.

After all the conferences were done, the teacher reviewed her notes and made a list of things that she needed to do with each child or watch for in a child. I thought they were very productive conferences and I thought Roberta had developed good relationships with these parents over the course of the school year. I can say that I really learned a great deal about parent-teacher relations in those two nights and one day.

In early childhood, if a teacher can assist a parent to see children's education positively, she can make a difference in the life of the child and the life of the family. When a teacher encourages and supports a parent's involvement in his child's schooling, the parent as well as the child stands to gain (Gorham & Nason, 1997). The parent's messages to the child about school are likely to be positive, and the child's comfort level at school is likely to be high: Greenberg's main point.

Parents in the Classroom

Nationally, Head Start has an enviable record of involving low-income, often minority group parents, in their children's education. Through home visits, support services, parents' meetings, advisory councils, and classroom volunteering, parents find new potential in themselves, personally, as parents, and even on occasion professionally. As a result of the Head Start experience, many parents begin career directions that simply had not occurred to them before. Certainly the child in Head Start, and often the whole family, benefit. With the current emphasis on academic readiness for Head Start children, this fundamental benefit too often is missed.

The importance of parent involvement, for the parent as well as the child, is clearly shown in this report by an experienced Head Start teacher in northern Minnesota:

OBSERVATION

On Wednesday, I had the opportunity to observe one of the Head Start parents volunteering in the classroom. It was 10:00 in the morning, during the children's free playtime. The mother that was volunteering decided that she would work with the kids at the "worm center." In the sensory table, the worm center had black dirt with live earthworms and plastic, nonliving earthworms. The children could work at the center if they wanted to, but they were not required to. Once the children saw there were living worms in the center, they were soon digging in the dirt.

For the first five or 10 minutes, Angela (the parent) just watched the children. This did not last long, however. Adam quickly got Angela involved when he put an earthworm in her hand and said, "Here's your worm."

Angela said, "Why thank you, Adam."

Nea looked at Angela and asked, "Do these worms live all over in the ground?"

Angela responded, "Yes they do, Nea, although they don't live in hot sandy places like the desert."

Nea then said, "Is that because it's too hot for them there?"

Angela responded, "Yep."

Adam then jumped in and said, "Know what, me and my Daddy go fishin with these, and we catch lots of big fish too."

Angela responded, "I'll bet you do, Adam, fish like to eat worms, don't they?"

Morgan came over to the table to see what was going on; she picked up a plastic worm and said, "This one's not moving."

Angela responded to Morgan's statement by asking her, "Is that a real worm, Morgan?"

Morgan looked at Angela with a confused look on her face. Angela waited a few moments so Morgan had some time to really think about what she asked. After a while Angela directed a second question at Morgan, "Do you know the difference between what is real and what isn't?"

Morgan looked at her and shook her head no. Angela then moved to the other end of the table so she could be by Morgan. Angela put a real worm in her right hand and plastic worm in her left hand. Angela then asked Morgan to look at the real worm and tell her what she saw. Morgan said, "The worm is moving."

Angela then told Morgan, "Now look at the worm in your other hand and tell me what you see."

Morgan said, "That worm doesn't move at all, not even when I touch it."

Angela then picked up an earthworm that had died and said, "Morgan, is this a real worm?"

Morgan looked at it and touched it and then she replied, "Yea, he's just dead." Angela looked at me and we both began to chuckle to ourselves.

REFLECTION

At the worm table Angela was able to observe first hand the learning that goes on during playtime. The children learned that worms live under the ground, but not in the desert. They also learned that worms are a food source for fish, and they worked on the concept of differentiating between what is real and what is not. Angela gained feelings of satisfaction from being able to help educate the children about worms. The children enjoyed her being there and she showed some real teaching skills.

This was the third time that I observed Angela volunteering in the classroom. I feel that she is participating at a very high level for two reasons. First is the comfort level that Angela displays when she is involved with the children. She interacts with them and directs stations without any hesitation. The second reason is that her son, Damien, is no longer by her side every waking moment that Angela is there, like he was the first time I observed her volunteering. I feel that her volunteering has helped both Damien and Angela grow in many ways.

In my university classes over the years, some of the most dedicated and responsive students have been parents of young children who chose teaching careers after finding their niche by volunteering in classrooms. In these encouraging classrooms, teachers were friendly enough to welcome them, help them find activities to do, thank them for volunteering, and invite them back. Finding the experience exhilarating, the parents returned. But, it is not solely to benefit the parents that teachers welcome them as classroom volunteers. It does not take a college degree to talk with a child, read a story, help with an interest center, present an activity, or assist with a trip. Parents who come into the classroom benefit programs in all of these ways. The teacher whose goal is to bridge home and school knows that the children, the educational program, and the teacher herself all gain when a parent comes to school.

Most especially, the child whose parent comes into the classroom gains. A well-known story is of an unemployed dad who accompanied his daughter one day to preschool. Unsure as he entered the classroom, the teacher welcomed him, introduced him to the children, and got him started reading stories. From the library corner Dad overheard three children, including his daughter, talking about what their parents did. One child said his dad was doctor. Another said her mom was a dentist. The man's daughter said with a big grin, "My Dad's here!"

PART FOUR: COMMUNICATING WITH PARENTS ABOUT GUIDANCE ISSUES

As teachers know, parents' views about their children and the subject of "discipline" vary a great deal: "My kid is basically a good kid who just needs some TLC." "My child can be willful and will try to get away with things unless you are right on him." Many of the expectations of parents go back to their own parents, and to the social, religious, and cultural views of their families. Once commonplace, the notion that children are to be "seen and not heard" has been replaced in many families by less authoritarian and more interactive parenting styles. Yet, the view that children are to be respectful of and compliant toward the adults in their lives is still held firmly by percentages of families in virtually any classroom. At the same time, some children come from home situations in which parents have not been able to establish consistent expectations at all.

In discussing children's behavior with parents, the teacher first seeks to understand how the parent views the child. The teacher works to be sensitive to differences in background that might make communication about the child more difficult. However else they differ, both parents and teacher share a priority for the well-being of the child. The teacher's job is to make the most of that common ground by remembering that whatever family values they espouse, parents want the best for their children (Gorham & Nason, 1997).

Parents who have positive views about their children generally accept the concept of mistaken behavior and its three levels. (See Chapter 2 for a review of the three levels of mistaken behavior.) Out of an adult sense of fair play, however, parents neither want their child "to get away with things" nor others to treat their child unfairly. In explaining behavior in terms of "making a mistake," the teacher needs to emphasize that the child is in a developmental process of learning more acceptable alternatives and that the teacher is providing guidance to help the child do so.

With relatively mild mistaken behavior, the teacher might say that she or he doubts that the behavior will occur again, but will continue to watch the situation. Especially with more serious behaviors, the teacher must be clear to the parent that children, like all of us, make mistakes. At the same time, the child needs to learn from the mistake, and the role of the teacher is to help. Calling a hurting or disruptive behavior "a mistake" does not justify it. Guidance is not necessarily permissive. In the terms of Haim Ginott, "Helpful correction is direction":

> Frank, age five, pinched his friend, Sam . . . The teacher who witnessed the event said to Frank, "I saw it. People are not for pinching." Frank said, "I am sorry." The teacher replied, "To be sorry is to make an inner decision to behave differently." "O.K.," replied Frank. He went over to Sam to resume his play. (1972, p. 129)

Although Frank may not have understood the teacher's exact words, he got the message. The teacher modeled guidance by being firm, not harsh, and by educating Frank about his actions.

The goal in communicating with the parent is to convey a stance of acceptance of the child and of appropriate guidance in relation to the child's behavior. The levels of mistaken behavior provide a helpful vocabulary for the teacher in working toward this goal. If a child is having problems, the teacher also needs to communicate about guidance tips, and especially about the effort, progress, and achievements the child has made. Parents, like all of us, accept suggestions for improvement more easily when progress is recognized first.

At times, parents will be more critical of the child than the teacher. Parents can express skepticism about their children's behaviors and still be nurturing parents. Occasionally, however, a teacher encounters a parent who has overly negative views about the child or unrealistic reactions to the child's mistaken behavior. One important comment needs to be made here. If a teacher believes that difficulties in parent-child communication are posing Level Three problems for the child, then the teacher needs to take a comprehensive problem-solving approach that includes collaboration with others (Nunnelly & Fields, 1999). (See Chapter 10 for further discussion of comprehensive guidance.) In collaboration with other professionals, the teacher works with the family to resolve the problem.

Communicating with Parents When There Are Disagreements

At one time or another, teachers and parents will experience differences in viewpoint about program priorities, program content, teaching style, behaviors of the parents' own children, or the behaviors of other children. Boutte, Keepler, Tyler, & Terry (1992), Galinsky (1988), Lightfoot (1978), and Powell (1989) make similar points about these disagreements: Teachers need to work to make differences *not* negative dissonances—which drive teacher and parent apart—but *creative conflicts*, which retain the possibility of being solved.

Lightfoot (1978) distinguishes between these terms by stating that **negative dissonance** is the result of differences that alienate the parent from the teacher. In such cases, the teacher typically asserts the power of the education institution over the parent, often on the basis of the parent's social or cultural background. Views, values, and communication styles of the parent are considered of lesser importance than those of the teacher, as an "official representative" of the school or center (Powell, 1989).

Creative conflicts arise from the diversity of life in a complex, pluralistic society in which the right of the individual to his or her own views is accepted (Lightfoot, 1978). The teacher who respects parents, whatever their background, realizes that disagreements in values or viewpoints need not terminate positive relations. The common ground of the child whose life they share makes differences into opportunities for creative communication and possible compromise, not inevitably points of division (Galinsky, 1988; Manning & Schindler, 1997).

Yet, the reality remains that some parents are difficult to communicate with, and many teachers feel unprepared for this part of their job

(Boutte et al., 1992). The tendency to support parents "selectively," depending on the teacher's feelings toward them, leads to the "negative dissonance" that is important to avoid (Powell, 1989).

In the article, "Effective Techniques for Involving 'Difficult' Parents," Boutte et al. (1992) provide suggestions for working with parents when conflicts arise. As a basic, teachers who find that they are in disagreement with parents use social problem solving, just as they would with children and fellow staff. (See Chapter Six for information about social problem solving techniques.) In addition, the following seven guidelines assist in a variety of situations when teacher and parents disagree:

1. *Encourage Mutual Respect.* Warren (1977) insightfully comments that parents who seem unworthy were themselves children whose unmet needs have prevented them from a healthy adulthood. The teacher who does not let personal judgments get in the way of involving parents in their children's education understands the importance of Warren's words.

   Parents from backgrounds different from the teacher's have legitimate points of pride and values that their children share. Remaining open to learning about the customs and lifestyles new to the teacher conveys respect for the family and the child.

   At the same time, the teacher can take pride in being a professional and need not be defensive about educational practice that she or he knows to be appropriate. Regardless of difference in age or experience, self-respect is a right of the early childhood teacher. As a professional, the teacher uses appropriate practice in relations with parents, no less than with children. Appropriate practice means an on going invitation to parents to become involved in the education process of the child (Rogers, Andre, & Hawley, 1996).

2. *Communicate with Staff and Consulting Professionals.* When a teacher detects a problem with a family, and certainly if a serious problem occurs, the teacher should discuss the situation with other staff (Rogers, Andre, & Hawley, 1996). The communication may range from asking for information from a colleague who knows the family to discussing the matter with an administrator. Venting to trusted others occasionally is important for the teacher's mental health, but communication about families needs to steer clear of the "teachers' lounge phenomenon" (carping and gossip). Beyond fellow staff, a consulting professional also can be a valuable resource (Manning & Schindler, 1997). In the complex world of today, teachers sometimes need collaboration with specialists to extend their ability to assist children and their families, and to learn and grow.

3. *Talk to the Situation.* In conferences about behaviors the teacher should have specific, objective information on hand about the child and the situation: anecdotal observations, dated time samples, and

perhaps journal entries by the child. The teacher describes events and does not judgmentally evaluate the child, the child's behavior, or the family background. The teacher also seeks information from the parent, Galinksy notes:

> Certain statements tend to create distrust and worry rather than an alliance. For example: If a teacher says, "Is something going on at home?" the parent may feel accused. Instead, try "Did Arthur have a hard time getting up today? He seems tired." (1988, p.11)

Basic guidance techniques like compliment sandwiches highlight progress and pose problems constructively. Honestly meant open-ended questions make conversations more friendly. A goal is to generate possible solutions for "creative conflicts" together, discussing the pros and cons of each (Rogers, Andre, & Hawley, 1996).

4. *Model Reflective Listening.* When parents feel strongly to the point of confrontation, the teacher needs to listen, allow them to cool off, and not dispute or "block out" what they say (Heath, 1994). To ensure the parent that the teacher is listening, she or he repeats the substance of what the parent has said, the basic element in reflective listening. The teacher is flexible about accepting specifics in the argument, but stops personal abuse, redirecting communication to the point of the meeting. Use of parents' ideas when deciding on follow-up shows that listening was at work. As part of the listening process, reiterating that everyone wants what is best for the child is important. Invitation for another contact in the future communicates that the teacher is serious about having parents involved. Parents who know they are being listened to become more likely to listen in return (Rogers, Andre, & Hawley, 1996).

5. *Invite Continued Involvement.* For parents who are assertive, the teacher works to accommodate their perspectives (Murphy, 1997). Positive strategies include providing current literature to discuss later, encouraging attendance at parent meetings, and seeking volunteer involvement in the classroom. Such measures give the parent a respectful opportunity to learn more about, and contribute to, the program. As Boutte et al. state:

> Parents usually will feel less alienated and will be more willing to participate if they are involved more in the decision-making regarding their children. All parents should be allowed to contribute to the program in some significant way. (1992, p. 20)

In inviting continued involvement in the child's education, the teacher makes hypotheses about the level and type of involvement the parent may accept. She or he adjusts expectations as necessary to keep the communication going. The teacher who works around a point of difference and wins an ally has truly mastered the principle of creative conflict resolution. (Manning & Schindler, 1997).

6. *Switch to Mediation.*   In some situations, conferences with parents do not work out successfully. In the event that productive communication grows impossible, the teacher takes the initiative to bring in a third party. The teacher may recognize this in the midst of a conference, in which case she usually terminates the conference and sets a process for rescheduling. A mediator makes it easier for all parties to understand that the disagreement is not a "personal grudge" or a personality conflict. When emotions are high, the mediator can help teacher and parent focus on the facts and decide on a strategy for positive resolution of the conflict (Koch & McDonough, 1999). Teachers sometimes feel that they are "failures" if they have to call on a third party. For the benefit of the child and maintaining relations with the family, this request is among the most professional a teacher can make.

7. *Collaborate for Safety.*   When dealing with serious family situations, the teacher may need to collaborate with colleagues for a reason beyond advice: for personal safety. In some circumstances, such as suspected child abuse, the teacher must report to authorities (Nunnelly & Fields, 1999). In rare occasions a teacher may feel a need to assist in an emergency, such as a battering or stalking situation. The teacher may feel vulnerable as a result of such acts.

The teacher is not a social worker, but is a member of a team of professionals helping the child and family. As soon as a problem appears more serious than the teacher handles in everyday duties, she or he needs to cease being the "point person" and collaborate with other staff and administration. Serious decisions regarding the health and safety of the child, or another member of a family served, must be made by a team led by a person trained in this area. Communication with the family at this point is to come not from the teacher, but from the appropriate team leader (Manning & Schindler, 1997).

Sometimes, in an effort to save a child from harm, the possible wrath of a family member must be risked. From the beginning of the child's time in the class, the teacher works with the family to prevent creative conflicts from becoming negative dissonances. In the event of a deteriorating situation, however, the teacher informs the principal or administrator and collaborates with others to prevent needlessly standing out and seeming responsible for an action.

When beginning in a new school or program, the teacher needs to determine the policy for handling serious situations. The teacher should discuss the policy with all parents as a part of a parent orientation or "greeting meeting." The teacher then follows the policy, gaining the assistance of other staff and administrators as necessary. When in doubt about a situation involving family members, collaborating with staff and supervisors is the key.

End Note: *The preceding chapter was compiled from the following: Gartrell, D. (2003).* A guidance approach for the encouraging classroom (3rd ed.). *Clifton Park, NY: Delmar Learning and Gartrell, D. J. (2000).* What the kids said today: *Using classroom conversations to become a better teacher, St. Paul, MN: Redleaf Press.*

REFERENCES

Boutte, G. S., Keepler, D. L., Tyler V. S., & Terry, B. Z (1992). Effective techniques for involving "difficult" parents. *Young Children, 47*(3), 32–37.

Curry, N. E., & Arnaud, S. H. (1995). Personality difficulties in preschool children as revealed through play themes and styles. *Young Children, 50*(4), 4–9.

Galinksy, E. (1988). Parents and teacher-caregivers: Sources of tension, sources of support. *Young Children, 43*(3), 4–12.

Gartrell, D. J. (2003). *A guidance approach for the encouraging classroom* (3rd ed.). Clifton Park, NY: Delmar Learning.

Ginott, H. (1972). *Teacher and child.* New York: Avon Books.

Gorham, P. J., & Nason, P. N. (1997). Why make teachers' work more visible to parents? *Young Children, 52*(5), 22–26.

Greenberg, P. (1989). Parents as partners in young children's development and education: A new American fad? Why does it matter? *Young Children, 44*(4), 61–75.

Heath, H. E. (1994). Dealing with difficult behaviors—Teachers plan with parents. *Young Children, 49*(5), 20–24.

Howard, S., Shaughnessy, A., Sanger, D., & Hux, K. (1998). Lets talk! Facilitating language in early elementary classrooms. *Young Children, 53*(3), 34–39.

Johnston, L., & Mermin, J. (1994). Easing children's entry to school: Home visits help. *Young Children, 49*(5), 62–68.

Koch, P. K., & McDonough, M. (1999). Improving parent-teacher conferences through collaborative conversations. *Young Children, 54*(2), 11–15.

Kratcoski, A. M., & Katz, K. B. (1998). Conversing with young language learners in the classroom. *Young Children, 53*(3), 30–33.

Lightfoot, S. L. (1978). *Worlds apart: Relationships between families and schools.* New York: Basic.

Locke, B. (1919, July). *Manufacturers indorse [sic] the kindergarten.* (Kindergarten Circular No. 4). Washington, DC: Department of the Interior, Bureau of Education.

Manning, D., & Schindler, P. J. (1997). Communicating with parents when their children have difficulties. *Young Children, 52*(5), 27–33.

Murphy, D. M. (1997). Parent and teacher plan for the child. *Young Children, 52*(4), 32–36.

Nunnelly, J. C., & Fields, T. (1999). Anger, dismay, guilt, anxiety—The realities and roles in reporting child abuse. *Young Children, 54*(5), 74–80.

Powell, D. R. (1989). *Families and early childhood programs.* Washington, DC: National Association for the Education of Young Children.

Rogers, R. E., Andre, L. C., & Hawley, M. K. (1996). *Parents and teachers as partners: Issues and challenges.* Fort Worth, TX: Houghton Mifflin.

Sandall, S., & Ostrosky, M. (Eds.). (1999). *Practical ideas for addressing challenging behaviors.* Denver, CO: Division for Early Childhood of the Council for Exceptional Children. (Available from NAEYC)

Stone, J. G. (2001). *Building classroom community: The early childhood teacher's role.* Washington, DC: NAEYC.

Taylor, J. (1999). Child-led parent/school conferences—In second grade?!? *Young Children, 54*(1), 78–81.

Warren, R. (1977). *Caring.* Washington, DC: National Association for the Education of Young Children.

Workman, S. H., & Gage, J. A. (1997). Family-school partnerships: A family strengths approach. *Young Children, 52*(4), 10–14.

Using Guidance to Build an Encouraging Classroom: Beyond Time-Out

QUICK TAKE

The first four chapters explored foundations of guidance. Key concepts were discussed; the importance of partnerships with families established. The remaining chapters further develop guidance ideas, but do so more as practices for direct classroom use. Chapter 5 is the first of a pair of articles from *Young Children* that examine alternatives to time-out; together they provide guidance strategies that make time-outs unnecessary.

Previous chapters argued that teachers use obedience-based discipline to keep children, literally and figuratively, in line. Perhaps the most discussed discipline technique in this traditional approach is the *time-out*. The assumption is that the teacher needs to use "time-out" to influence children to participate in the established educational program. Children who don't "get with the program" are threatened with temporary expulsion from the group (which is what time out is).

The dangers in this view are that (1) young children too often threatened with temporary expulsion tend over time to become permanently alienated; and (2) punitive discipline used to justify educational practices that are not developmentally appropriate causes young children to dislike their classroom situations and even disassociate from the learning process.

In contrast, *guidance* has a definite, proactive outcome: the teaching of *democratic life skills* (the skills needed to be healthy individuals and productive citizens in a democracy). This chapter argues that a priority of education should be teaching democratic life skills (more than an emphasis on test scores or other artifacts of political accountability). As they emphasize practices that teach democratic life skills—and children are not threatened with removal from the group—teachers' programs become fundamentally more educational and their classrooms become more encouraging.

Teachers often hear that time-outs do not help children's development and learning. Less often they are given reasons why. Less often still do teachers receive specific information about what works instead. This chapter explains "what the fuss is about" concerning time-outs and why it is important to replace time-outs with guidance that builds an encouraging classroom.

Confusion about time-out is understandable, as experts still disagree about its use (Schreiber, 1999; Ucci, 1998). Time-out probably was first used as a classroom alternative to embarrassment, scolding, and corporal punishment. Caring teachers wanted other means for dealing with classroom conflicts, and time-out became the commonly used alternative.

There has always been ambiguity about the use of this technique. When a teacher removes a child from a situation and helps the child calm down so the two can then talk about and, hopefully, resolve the conflict, the intervention is often positive, leading to important learning. Most of us have difficulty negotiating when we are upset. But in many classrooms a child is removed to a chair or unoccupied part of the room as a consequence of something he or she has done. Virtually all early childhood educators now believe that a child should never be put in complete isolation (Ucci, 1998), although some still are in favor of disciplining a child through the use of time-out. Ucci (1998) gives the rationale that to gain control, a child needs to be removed from a conflict so the child can think about his or her behavior and figure out what to do.

Ucci argues that the use of all discipline, including the time-out, "should be viewed not as punishment, but rather as supportive of and teaching about how to gain [behavioral] control and express feelings appropriately" (2003, p. 3). From this perspective, the time-out is a logical consequence of a child's losing control in a situation or otherwise acting inappropriately.

The usual length of the time-out is a minute or two for a toddler and five to 10 minutes for an older child. With preschoolers, teachers sometimes use a timer to help them recognize that the time-out will have a definite end (Ucci, 1998). In contrast, teachers who disagree with time-out as a discipline technique sometimes use the term *cooling down time,* when referring to removal that will help a child calm down so a conflict can be resolved (Gartrell, 2003).

WHAT THE FUSS IS ABOUT

When used as discipline, the time-out is one of a group of techniques—including the name-on-the-board, an assigned yellow or red "light," and the disciplinary referral slip—that still rely on blame and shame to bring a child's behavior "back into line." (Perhaps the most odious is putting a child on specially made green, yellow, and red steps, depending on frequency of the conflicts. This is the modern equivalent of the dunce stool.) One of the problems with these techniques, seen by some adults as "logical consequences," is that generally they are more logical to the adult than to the child. Although the adult's intent is to discipline rather than punish, children tend to perceive these traditional discipline techniques as "the infliction of pain and suffering," which is, in fact, a fairly standard definition of punishment.

Going back to the 19th century, early childhood writers have criticized discipline techniques that punish children rather than positively teach them (Gartrell, 2003). Froebel went so far as to say that through punishment, adults can make a child "bad" (as cited in Lilley, 1967). Montessori (1912/1964) decried traditional systems that reward and punish rather than teach children how to discipline themselves. More recently, Katz (1984) has argued that punishments such as time-outs confuse young children because they cannot easily understand the sequence of behaviors during and after a conflict nor what removal to a chair has to do with them. Clewett (1988) has pointed out that such punishments discourage the individual child and dampen the spirit of all children in the class. Marion (1999) explains that the time-out is "punishment by loss," meaning that the adult temporarily deprives the child of membership in the group and, as a punishment, "does not teach."

Referring especially to toddlers, Schreiber offers five reasons why the time-out is an undesirable practice:

1. The imposed external control of the time-out inhibits a child's ability to build internal controls and may cause a child lasting feelings of "being ineffectual."

2. The child placed on a time-out chair does not have personal needs met, including the need to develop alternative strategies.

3. The time-out diminishes the child's developing self-worth and self-confidence; it may cause others to view the child as a troublemaker.

4. The young child has difficulty understanding the relation of actions to consequences and may feel bewildered by the time-out experience.

5. Opportunities for learning valuable lessons in social relations are lost during the period of isolation, [and humiliation from the time-out may diminish the value of adult follow-up]. (1999, pp. 22–23)

In my view, these considerations apply to older children as well.

Clewett (1988) points out that an air of discouragement pervades a classroom in which a time-out chair is prominent. Teachers in such classrooms have institutionalized *conditional acceptance*, with adult rejection an ever-lingering threat if rules are disobeyed. A child placed on the chair experiences public loss of group membership. Other children become apprehensive that they may be the next to be excluded from the group. When conditional acceptance becomes the routine, in-groups and out-groups tend to form. Too often, institutions perpetuate this undesirable social dynamic, to the loss of all and the considerable detriment of some.

In addition to the writers cited above, the NAEYC Code of Ethical Conduct (NAEYC, 1998) and the NAEYC publication *Developmentally Appropriate Practice in Early Childhood Programs* (Bredekamp & Copple, 1997) advocate use of positive discipline or guidance. The difference between guidance and traditional discipline can be summarized this way:

> Traditional classroom discipline too easily slides into punishment; it punishes children for making mistakes in their behavior. Guidance rejects the pain and suffering involved in punishment. Guidance teaches children to solve their problems, rather than punishing them for having problems they cannot solve. Guidance teaches children to learn from their mistakes rather than "disciplining" children for the mistakes they make. (Gartrell, 1997)

In addition to replacing time-out, we need to replace all discipline techniques that impose pain and suffering. Instead, teachers can focus on four positive and instructive practices: being a guidance professional, teaching democratic life skills, using leadership communication,* and building an encouraging program.

A GUIDANCE PROFESSIONAL

Time-outs often provide noticeable short-term benefits, which can be more obvious than the negative side effects. It takes commitment, time, and effort to learn guidance alternatives and, until a teacher masters them, they may seem less effective (Da Ros & Kovach 1998). To learn and use effective alternatives, teachers must be **guidance professionals.**

It is never too late to become a guidance professional. (A model teacher, in her late forties, once told me it took five years before she felt her guidance responses had become automatic.) In my experience, after learning to use guidance effectively, even veteran teachers wonder how they ever managed before. This anecdote illustrates how one kindergarten teacher moved toward professionalism.

A n e c d o t e

> Early in the year, Jamal got upset with another child and punched her in the stomach. The teacher became furious and marched him to the time-out chair. Later in the day the principal gave Jamal a stern lecture. Two days later, Jamal got into another argument and hit again. As the teacher came toward him, Jamal walked to the time-out chair by himself and said, "I know. I'm going 'cause I'm no good." The teacher knelt beside him, put her arm around his shoulders, and explained that he did not upset her but that his behavior did. Afterward, she worked to improve their relationship. (Gartrell, 2003, p. 122)

When the teacher used the time-out with Jamal, she did not try to figure out all that happened, how Jamal saw the problem, what alternatives he might learn for next time, and how he might make amends for his actions and rejoin the group. Instead, she reacted to a hard-and-fast rule—zero tolerance for aggression—with the established response: time-out and a stern lecture.

The teacher's own sense of ethics prompted her to move toward professionalism. When the second incident occurred, she realized that punishment was having a negative effect on Jamal's self-concept. In a

---

*The section, Leadership Communication, did not appear in the original *Young Children* article.

meeting with staff who knew Jamal, she learned that after living in foster homes, he and his siblings had just been returned to their mother's care. The mother had been working hard to overcome chemical dependency.

The teacher began getting to know Jamal so she could better understand him and his behavior. She changed her morning routine to share 10 minutes alone with him every day. Her assistant helped make it possible to dedicate this time to Jamal, and both teachers became more encouraging of Jamal's everyday activities.

They also helped Jamal develop and use a strategy that allowed him to sense when he was losing control and remove himself from conflicts. One day, Jamal walked away from a conflict and, very upset, approached the teacher. She suggested he go into the bathroom, shut the door, and spit in the sink for as long as he wanted. I arrived to see a thirsty little boy come out of the bathroom and head straight for the water fountain! After the teacher quickly washed out the sink, she had a quiet talk with him about the conflict.

Teacher-child attachments are necessary if a child is to trust enough to learn to manage classroom conflicts (Betz, 1994). In conflict situations the guidance professional acts as a mediator, seeking to understand the situation and lead children toward peaceable resolution. This use of conflict management teaches children important life skills. When teachers use time-out, they often think they are shaming the child into "being good." The truth is that young children have not yet mastered the complex life skills of expressing strong emotions, resolving social problems peaceably, and getting along. The teacher may think that the child knows better and has only to be reminded. But the child is *just beginning* to build understandings and learn communication techniques that, in fact, some adults never learn, and most of us learn only imperfectly (Gartrell, 1995).

While shame may cause the child to halt (or at least be more careful about) the immediate behavior, it does nothing to teach positive alternative behaviors. Shaming also has psychological side effects. The child feels like a failure because he does not know something the teacher expects him to know (Clewett, 1988; Schreiber, 1999). And shame reinforces a negative self-fulfilling prophecy. This likely was happening for Jamal, who already saw himself as "no good." If a child internalizes a negative label, preconsciously he is going to ask a natural follow-up question, "How do bad kids act?" In answering this question, children like Jamal often have *more* conflicts than before the traditional discipline was applied—and the negative self-label introduced (Gartrell, 1995). These reasons account at least in part for the fact that for many children, time-out does not work (Betz, 1994; Clewett, 1988). Think about it: a pattern of "I do something bad; therefore I am punished; therefore I am bad; therefore I do something bad" is not a life pattern we want to reinforce!

DEMOCRATIC LIFE SKILLS

These days, most things educational are expected to have goals, standards, or outcomes. With traditional discipline, the goal is obvious: an orderly classroom with children literally and figuratively kept in line (as the saying goes, "The teacher teaches and the students learn"). The expectation is that from compliance in childhood comes character in adulthood.

The problem with this goal is that it reflects a time in our society when children were "seen and not heard." In years past (before Drs. Spock and Brazelton, among others) most families tended to have authoritarian parenting styles, with parents in charge and the "goodness" of children evaluated by how well they obeyed. But today's children come more often from families with different values and interaction patterns. More so than in the past, even very young children make real choices and express thoughts freely. For many families parent-driven rules and punishments are reserved for a relatively small number of situations. Practices like parent-child "chats" and family meetings are on the increase. Aware as well that they should not be overly permissive, these parents work hard to be not permissive but interactive, not authoritarian but authoritative.

At the same time it is now well known that some children also come from families under stress. Their parents for various reasons are unable to provide the healthy attachments and encouragement that young children need. Children like Jamal often enter classrooms unsure of how to behave with others, especially adults.

In this complex new culture, effective teachers need to be leaders, not bosses. In Piaget's (1932/1960) words, they must work for the goal of "autonomy" (intelligent and ethical decision making) rather than obedience. For many years, educators such as Dewey (1900/1969), Piaget (1932/1960), and Dreikurs (1968) argued for this shift in teaching priorities. In recent years, educators such as Katz (as cited in Kantrowitz & Wingert, 1989), Elkind (1997), and Gardner (1993) have expressed similar views.

The goals of *guidance* come from many sources. For Dewey (1916/1945), the purpose of education was full and productive involvement in the perpetuation of democracy. Piaget (1932/1960) said education should lead to *autonomy.* Gardner (1993) believes healthy development includes *interpersonal and intrapersonal intelligences,* the capacity to understand one's own needs and emotions and to balance this knowledge with responsiveness to the perspectives of others. And Katz (as cited in Kantrowitz & Wingert, 1989) says that in addition to the traditional Three Rs, children need to learn the lessons of a new "first" R: *relationships.*

According to these thinkers and others, and the NAEYC Code of Ethical Conduct (NAEYC, 1998), the goals of guidance can be stated in terms of **democratic life skills**—the abilities children need to function as productive citizens and healthy individuals.

Democratic life skills include the ability to

- see one's self as a worthy individual and a capable member of the group.
- express strong emotions in nonhurting ways.
- solve problems ethically and intelligently.
- be understanding of the feelings and viewpoints of others.
- work cooperatively in groups, with acceptance of the human differences among members. (Gartrell, 2003)

Teaching democratic life skills is not a diversion from "real teaching," but integral to it. We teach these skills not just through conflicts resolved peaceably but also through the curriculum. In addition, guidance professionals actively model and teach democratic life skills throughout every day. They expect children to learn them, and guide them in the process. Such teachers see conflict not as the result of misbehavior, but of *mistaken behavior,* from which the child can learn (Gartrell, 1995). While teachers can reduce mistaken behaviors through use of developmentally appropriate practice, they recognize that conflicts happen every day. The challenge for teachers—and children—is to recognize conflicts as opportunities for teaching and learning.

A commitment to guidance includes viewing curriculum as something that is a part of children's lives. Education is about learning to live together peaceably and solving problems cooperatively and creatively— more so than preparation for standardized tests and drills in basic skills. Each time children are helped to resolve conflicts, they engage in high-level social studies, language arts, and sometimes even mathematical thinking. I once heard a four-year-old exclaim, "I am so 'frusticated', I got to get the teacher to help us share!" The teacher did help, and gently reinforced the word *frustrated.*

It is important to see children who experience repeated, serious conflicts not as problem children but as children with problems who need guidance. Such children sometimes need comprehensive guidance to resolve issues that are bigger than they are. With both children who experience typical conflicts and those who have serious problems due to unmet needs, alternatives to traditional discipline can help them, and others in the class, build democratic life skills. Professional teachers use guidance to ensure that no child is stigmatized and denied full membership in the classroom community and so that all children progress in the use and learning of democratic life skills (Gartrell, 2003).

LEADERSHIP COMMUNICATION

Some communication techniques work better than others at helping teachers be guidance professionals and teach democratic life skills. In fact, some accepted practices, like making clear rules and giving frequent praise, are less helpful than teachers think. This section discusses communication techniques that establish the teacher as a friendly leader in the task of building an encouraging classroom. The discussion illustrates techniques teachers use to create a spirit of community in the classroom—reducing the need for many mistaken behaviors. A full treatment of these techniques, and others, can be found in Chapters 7 and 8 of my textbook (2003), on which this section is based.

1. Guidelines Not Rules

Marlys, with some water on her shirt, complains that Kiko has broken the rule, "no splashing at the water table." The teacher feels obligated to move Kiko to another center. When Kiko, with a soaked front, says Marlys dumped water on him first, the teacher moves both children. The two children sulk—they have not been helped to solve their problem or learn how to play together at the water table. They are likely feeling "unworthy" because they "broke the rule."

Rules tend to be stated in negative terms: "No running in the classroom"; "No 'naughty words' at school." Often rules come with pre-set consequences:

- No talking during lessons or your name goes on the board.
- Children who hurt others sit on the time-out chair.
- If your homework is not done, you stay in at recess.

The conventional thinking about rules is that they set clear conditions of citizenship in the class and teach that actions have consequences. This viewpoint presents difficulties for teachers who wish to create encouraging classrooms.

Because of lack of experience and development, children have particular reactions to rules that adults may not anticipate. Children may think that a teacher's emphasis on rules means he expects the children to break them—not a wholesome classroom atmosphere. If they do break a rule, young children have difficulty understanding that the punishment is the result of their specific actions. They tend instead to internalize a general sense of shame and see themselves as "bad children." Children have then been influenced away from feelings of initiative, belonging, and industry—and toward shame and self-doubt (Elkind, 1997).

Rules tend to institutionalize the use of punishment in the classroom. Formalized rules affect the way teachers see their jobs. If a rule is broken, the teacher must enforce it, or risk looking inconsistent. Often teachers do not know the "whole story" when they intervene. Rather than seek to understand and solve the problem, a rule-oriented environment pressures teachers to act like technicians, making a swift judgment based on too little or even biased information. The teacher's reactions in the preceding anecdote illustrate this situation.

Like rules, **guidelines** set standards for the classroom, but unlike rules, guidelines reinforce these standards in a positive way. Rather than threaten exclusion, guidelines teach what children can do to fit into, and participate as a member of, the class. Guidelines provide proactive, concrete lessons that tell the child "You can do this." "You can learn to get along in our classroom."

The following list of primary-grade guidelines can be reduced and adapted for younger children. Even at the preschool level, the teacher can formulate guidelines such as these with the class and can use them as reminders and teaching points with children, both individually and in groups.

- Friendly touches only
- We use words to solve our problems
- Sometimes we need to stop, look, and listen
- We all help to take care of our room
- We are friendly to each other and to ourselves
- Making mistakes is OK—we just try to learn from them

Guidelines encourage the teacher to be understanding rather than patient; a professional rather than a technician; an adult who helps Marlys and Kiko learn to play together in the water table, rather than expel them from it. Guidelines, rather than traditional rules, set the tone for the encouraging classroom.

2. Encouragement Not Praise

Teachers often hear that "praise is good." But the following two anecdotes illustrate common problems with praise when it is conventionally given. Many teachers use a series of stock phrases that are really "mental shortcuts" for keeping routines and practices going. Adjectives like "good" and "nice" often are a part of these phrases, which over time have little meaning for children and even less for the teacher.

Teachers often use praise in social situations to manipulate the group by pointing out positive "models." This practice sets up "winners" and "losers" in the class, and works against an encouraging classroom in which

> A teacher went down the row of kindergarten children working on their pictures. As she passed by each she said, "Good job," "Good job." A child at the end of the row complained, "Teacher, you say that all the time."

all children feel they are valued uniquely but equally as contributing members.

Praise tends to publicly single out achievements, implicitly making comparisons to the efforts of others. *Encouragement,* in contrast to praise, tends to authentically acknowledge ongoing progress—when children most need kind words—and avoids evaluative comparisons. Two kinds of encouragement steer the teacher toward helpful communication:

Public encouragement does not single out individuals, but acknowledges the efforts of an entire group. "You all are working so hard that we will have colorful pictures up all over the room." "You are sitting so still today, just like Snoopy statues. Everyone who is wearing blue or brown can quietly line up." Public encouragement, directed to the whole group, builds group spirit among all the members of the class.

Private encouragement is directed to the individual, quietly, so the child knows it is meant just for her. Teachers often say "good job" to individual children because it is easier than figuring out what else to say.

The secret to effective private encouragement (like public encouragement) is to pick out details and compliment them. Two simple *starter statements* (used separately or together) are

> At the end of a large-group activity, a prekindergarten teacher picked Melissa to lead the line, because he said, "Melissa is sitting just right with her mouth closed up tight." A few children muttered, "I was sitting good too." "Teacher always picks Melissa." "I never get to lead." Some children did sit straighter and "lock" their lips. Others just sat as if they knew they wouldn't be picked any time soon.

"You are really . . . ."

"You sure are . . . ."

Stock statements of praise tend to shortcut conversation—not a lot a child can say to "nice picture" (especially if the child doesn't think it is "nice"). Thoughtful encouragement often results in friendly conversation—friendly because the child appreciates that the teacher cared enough to pay attention to her work: "I am making this picture for you, teacher."

Teachers who use guidelines, public encouragement, and private encouragement have the foundation of communication skills to build an

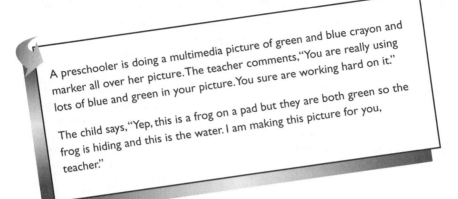

A preschooler is doing a multimedia picture of green and blue crayon and marker all over her picture. The teacher comments, "You are really using lots of blue and green in your picture. You sure are working hard on it."

The child says, "Yep, this is a frog on a pad but they are both green so the frog is hiding and this is the water. I am making this picture for you, teacher."

encouraging classroom. The following table shows five additional techniques that offer alternatives and possibilities for helping each child feel accepted as a member of the classroom community. All of these techniques take commitment and practice, but together they define much of the friendly communication that is present when teachers are building classrooms where people care.

Five Teacher Communication Skills For Building The Encouraging Classroom

Communication Skill	Suggestions for Use
Listening to life experiences Purpose: to reduce stress levels child brings into classroom that may prevent productive behavior	1. Greet children individually to assess comfort—stress levels. 2. Make time to listen to children in need as soon as possible after arrival. 3. Use reflective listening to affirm child's thoughts and feelings.
Contact talks Purpose: to enable child and teacher to get to know each other beyond classroom routines	1. Use chart of names to assure contact talks with all on regular basis. 2. Establish physical proximity in a relaxed manner to ensure talk occurs. 3. Follow child's lead; discuss what is interesting to child to talk about.

continued

Five Teacher Communication Skills For Building
The Encouraging Classroom—*continued*

Communication Skill	Suggestions for Use
Compliment sandwiches Purpose: to guide individual to productive behavior by giving encouragement for effort and progress already evident and directing to further progress	1. Start transaction with one (better two) positive comments about effort or progress the child has shown. 2. Offer one specific suggestion or request for continued progress for each set of compliments given. 3. End transaction again with one or two compliments.
Friendly Humor Purpose: to experience and share enjoyable moments with children and fellow adults	1. Seek to enjoy the unexpected in words, behaviors, and situations. 2. Share delightful moments with children and adults in friendly ways that laugh "with" and not "at."
Friendly Touch Purpose: to provide reassurance and affirmation to children in ways that words cannot	1. Discuss, set, know, and follow policies in the school or program regarding the use of touch with children. 2. Discuss and reach understandings about touch with parents. 3. Respect individual children's needs for touch and for personal space.

AN ENCOURAGING PROGRAM

In the encouraging classroom, teachers work together in teams to make the schedule responsive to the rhythms of the group; provide an environment that encourages individual and small-group engagement; adjust the curriculum to children's attention spans, learning styles, and family backgrounds; and include democratic life skills in the curriculum. By using practices that are developmentally appropriate and culturally responsive, teaching teams reduce the kinds of institutionally caused conflicts that children do not cause so much as fall into. At the same time, the team recognizes that there are other conflicts that occur in even the most encouraging classroom environments. When many small bodies are in a small space for long hours with few adults, conflicts happen.

Teachers in encouraging classrooms work hard to reduce the frequency of conflicts caused by an inappropriate environment or activities. They continuously review and modify the daily schedule, classroom lay-

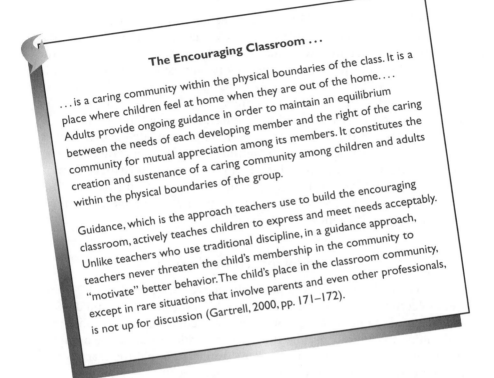

The Encouraging Classroom ...

... is a caring community within the physical boundaries of the class. It is a place where children feel at home when they are out of the home. ... Adults provide ongoing guidance in order to maintain an equilibrium between the needs of each developing member and the right of the caring community for mutual appreciation among its members. It constitutes the creation and sustenance of a caring community among children and adults within the physical boundaries of the group.

Guidance, which is the approach teachers use to build the encouraging classroom, actively teaches children to express and meet needs acceptably. Unlike teachers who use traditional discipline, in a guidance approach, teachers never threaten the child's membership in the community to "motivate" better behavior. The child's place in the classroom community, except in rare situations that involve parents and even other professionals, is not up for discussion (Gartrell, 2000, pp. 171–172).

out, and curriculum. They practice positive leadership through the communication skills they use.

Daily Schedule

The daily schedule for a Head Start class called for returning to the classroom after active play, lining up for bathroom and hand-washing, and then sitting down for lunch. After one month, the teachers noticed the children had problems waiting in line, with conflicts occurring almost daily. They met to discuss the problem and plan a different approach. The class was already divided into four family groups, each led by a member of the teaching team. On a rotating basis, one family group came in early to help prepare the tables and get themselves ready for lunch. When the other groups returned to the classroom, the children went to the library corner to look at books individually and in pairs. The teacher would have a few children at a time go to the bathroom to wash hands and transition to the lunch tables. Everyone would eat lunch with his or her family group. From the first day teachers tried the new approach, conflicts clearly diminished.

Room Arrangement

In a kindergarten class of 24 children, centers for reading, house, and blocks and trucks were set up around the edges of the room. The teacher observed that the centers were too crowded, and some children used the large open area in the middle of the room as a raceway for the trucks. In fact, a couple of the boys referred to this space as the "track." After attending a workshop on learning centers, the teacher added centers for writing, art, music, science, and technology. He spaced them around the room to eliminate runways, clustering them by estimated activity levels. For daily work time he asked the children to decide what centers they intended to use and they recorded their choices in journals (with early writing and art). Children's playtime soon became more productive, and the teacher began to weave center use into math and language arts focus times and periodic themes.

Modifying Curriculum

A first-year teacher planned a pumpkin activity for her class of 21 children. Everyone sat in a circle and each child in turn came up and dug out one spoonful of pulp from the pumpkin. The children soon became restless waiting for their turns, and the teacher decided to carve the pumpkin herself. A mother later saw the jack-o'-lantern and told the teacher that her family did not recognize or celebrate Halloween.

The next year the teacher again planned a pumpkin activity but changed it to make it more appropriate and effective. The teacher, her assistant, and two parent volunteers divided the class into four groups for a visit to the pumpkin patch, where each group picked a pumpkin. Back in the classroom, the children worked on their pumpkins in small groups. They were actively involved and had few conflicts. One group of children and a parent whom the teacher knew did not celebrate Halloween, cut their pumpkin into small pieces and made pumpkin bars and collected the seeds for roasting. The teacher concluded that the revised activity was much more developmentally appropriate and culturally responsive, *and* it minimized conflicts.

Developing Curriculum

At the beginning of the year, a preschool teaching team developed themes based on democratic life skills. As part of the theme for "work cooperatively in groups," the teachers put on a puppet play about two bears who would not let a frog play with them. The teachers stopped the play and invited the children to discuss what had happened. Using the children's ideas, the teachers revised the play—this time the bears let the frog play with them. The children were much happier with this ending.

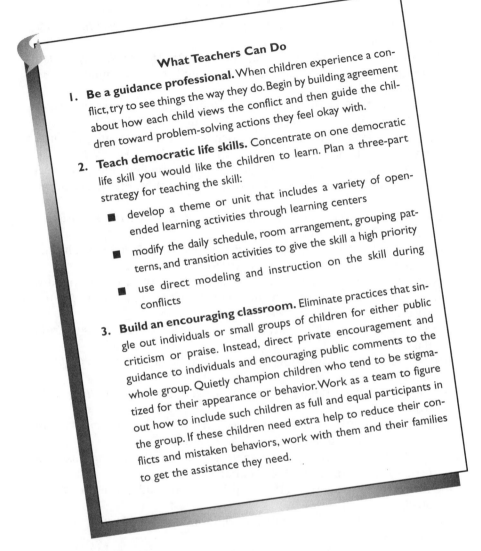

What Teachers Can Do

1. **Be a guidance professional.** When children experience a conflict, try to see things the way they do. Begin by building agreement about how each child views the conflict and then guide the children toward problem-solving actions they feel okay with.

2. **Teach democratic life skills.** Concentrate on one democratic life skill you would like the children to learn. Plan a three-part strategy for teaching the skill:

   - develop a theme or unit that includes a variety of open-ended learning activities through learning centers

   - modify the daily schedule, room arrangement, grouping patterns, and transition activities to give the skill a high priority

   - use direct modeling and instruction on the skill during conflicts

3. **Build an encouraging classroom.** Eliminate practices that single out individuals or small groups of children for either public criticism or praise. Instead, direct private encouragement and guidance to individuals and encouraging public comments to the whole group. Quietly champion children who tend to be stigmatized for their appearance or behavior. Work as a team to figure out how to include such children as full and equal participants in the group. If these children need extra help to reduce their conflicts and mistaken behaviors, work with them and their families to get the assistance they need.

In encouraging classrooms all children find a welcome place. The teaching team works continuously to make the program responsive to each child in the group. Children learn to manage their conflicts without bullying and other forms of violence (Carlsson-Paige & Levin, 2000). The teachers are positive leaders who continue to learn even as they teach. They have become guidance professionals who help children learn democratic life skills.

End Note: *The preceding chapter appeared in the November 2001 issue of* Young Children *under the original title: "Replacing Time Out: Part One—Using Guidance to Build the Encouraging Classroom. Gartrell, D. J. (2001).* Young Children *56(6) 8–16.*

REFERENCES

Betz, C. (1994). Beyond time-out: Tips from a teacher. *Young Children, 49* (3), 10–14.

Bredekamp, S., & Copple, C. (Eds.). (1997). *Developmentally appropriate practice in early childhood programs* (Rev. ed.). Washington, DC: NAEYC.

Carlsson-Paige, N., & Levin, D. E. (2000). *Before push comes to shove: Building conflict resolution skills with children.* St. Paul, MN: Redleaf Press.

Clewett, A. S. (1988). Guidance and discipline: Teaching young children appropriate behavior. *Young Children, 43* (4), 25–36.

Da Ros, D. A., & Kovach, B. A. (1998). Assisting toddlers and caregivers during conflict resolutions: Interactions that promote socialization. *Childhood Education, 75* (1), 25–30.

Dewey, J. (1969). *The school and society.* New York: Free Press. (Original work published 1900)

Dewey, J. (1945). *Democracy and education.* Chicago: University of Chicago Press. (Original work published 1916)

Dreikurs, R. (1968). *Psychology in the classroom.* New York: Harper & Row.

Elkind, D. (1997, November). The death of child nature: Education in the postmodern world. *Phi Delta Kappan,* 241–245.

Gardner, H. (1993). *Multiple intelligences: The theory in practice.* New York: Basic.

Gartrell, D. J. (1995). Misbehavior or mistaken behavior? *Young Children, 50* (5), 27–34.

Gartrell, D. J. (1997). Beyond discipline to guidance. *Young Children, 52* (6), 34–42.

Gartrell, D. J. (2000). *What the kids said today: Using classroom conversations to become a better teacher.* St. Paul, MN: Redleaf.

Gartrell, D. J. (2003). *A guidance approach for the encouraging classroom* (3rd ed.). Clifton Park, NY: Delmar Learning.

Kantrowitz, B., & Wingert, P. (1989, April 17). How kids learn. *Newsweek,* 50–56.

Katz, L. (1984). The professional early childhood teacher. *Young Children, 39* (5), 3–10.

Lilley, I. M., (Ed.). (1967). *Friedrich Froebel: A selection from his writings.* London: Cambridge University Press.

Marion, M. (1999). *Guidance of young children.* New York: Merrill.

Montessori, M. (1964). *The Montessori method.* New York: Shocken Books. (Original work published 1912)

NAEYC. (1998). *Code of ethical conduct and statement of commitment.* [Brochure]. Washington, DC: Author.

Piaget, J. (1960). *The moral judgment of the child.* Glencoe, IL: Free Press. (Original work published 1932)

Schreiber, M. E. (1999). Time-outs for toddlers: Is our goal punishment or education? *Young Children, 54* (4), 22–25.

Ucci, M. (1998). "Time outs" and how to use them. *Child Health Alert* (1), 2–3.

FOR FURTHER READING

Beane, A. L. (2000). *The bully free classroom.* Minneapolis: Free Spirit.

Elkind, D. (1997, November). The death of child nature: Education in the postmodern world. *Phi Delta Kappan,* 241–245.

Froschl, M., & Sprung, B. (1999). On purpose: Addressing teasing and bullying in early childhood. *Young Children, 54* (2), 70–72.

Harris, T. T., & Fuqua, J. D. (2000). What goes around comes around: Building a community of learners through circle times. *Young Children, 55* (1), 44–47.

Kaiser, B., & Rasminsky, J. (1999). *Meeting the challenge: Effective strategies for challenging behaviours in early childhood environments.* Ottawa, Ontario, Canada: Canadian Child Care Federation. (Available from NAEYC)

Lawhon, T. (1997). Encouraging friendships among children. *Childhood Education, 73* (4), 228–231.

Logan, T. (1998). Creating a kindergarten community. *Young Children, 53* (2), 22–26.

Marion, M. (1997). Guiding young children's understanding and management of anger. *Young Children, 52* (7), 62–67.

McClurg, L. G. (1998). Building an ethical community in the classroom: Community meeting. *Young Children, 53* (2), 30–35.

Nansel, T. R., Overpeck, M., Pilla, R. S., Ruan, W. J., Simons-Morton, B., & Scheidt, P. (2001). Bullying behaviors among U.S. youth: Prevalence and association with psychosocial adjustment. *Journal of the American Medical Association, 285* (16), 2094–2100.

Sandall, S., & Ostrosky, M. (Eds). (1999). *Practical ideas for addressing challenging behaviors.* Denver, CO: Division for Early Childhood of the Council for Exceptional Children. (Available from NAEYC)

Stone, J. G. (2001). *Building classroom community: The early childhood teacher's role.* Washington, DC: NAEYC.

CHAPTER 6

Using Guidance to Maintain an Encouraging Classroom: Four Intervention Alternatives

QUICK TAKE

The encouraging classroom, one could say, is a place where children want to be when they are sick, instead of not wanting to be there when they are well. A major challenge for teachers is how to maintain an encouraging classroom when mistaken behavior happens. The measure of the teacher's commitment to guidance is the ability to show authoritative leadership, intervening when needed in firm but friendly ways and protecting the guidelines of the classroom community.

This chapter continues the discussion of alternatives to time-out by presenting four intervention strategies for when children experience classroom conflicts that they cannot solve. All four practices model and teach social problem solving, the basis of teacher intervention in encouraging classrooms. *Conflict management* is used when a small number of children cannot resolve a conflict on their own. *Guidance talks* are appropriate when the conflict centers around one child. *Class meetings* are useful when conflicts are very public and involve many children in the group. *Comprehensive guidance* is necessary when a child shows recurrent, strong-needs mistaken behavior. Conflict management is the gold standard of guidance interventions in the encouraging classroom and is the featured strategy of the chapter.

The previous chapter argues that time-out, as a typical form of traditional classroom discipline, punishes children for making mistakes in their behavior. As punishment, time-out does not help young children learn positive alternatives from their mistakes (Schreiber, 1999). In the guidance approach, teachers build encouraging classrooms that reduce mistaken behavior by holding developmentally appropriate expectations, using friendly communication, and teaching democratic life skills.

Chapter 6 extends the discussion of the encouraging classroom by addressing conflicts (when children experience definite disagreements) and often resulting mistaken behavior. Some adults use guidance only in mild conflict situations, such as two children arguing over who has the larger piece of play dough. These adults believe that when conflicts are more serious—such as one child pushing another off a chair to grab the play dough—"discipline" becomes necessary. This chapter might well be subtitled "All Guidance, All the Time."

A MODEL FOR SOCIAL PROBLEM SOLVING

The guidance alternative to traditional discipline is social problem solving. The premise of social problem solving is that because young children are just beginning the process of learning democratic life skills, they naturally make mistakes. Adults use social problem solving to teach children the democratic life skills they need to learn from their mistakes (Gartrell, 2001).

The second part of the chapter explains four basic guidance techniques that together sustain encouraging preschool and elementary classrooms, places where all children feel welcome despite the conflicts that some experience. All four techniques use the process of social problem solving. They help teachers refrain from making moral judgments about children so they can focus instead on teaching the democratic life skills children need to be productive citizens and healthy individuals.

The four guidance basics are:

■ **classic conflict management**

Used when two or more children experience conflict with one another, such as two children aggressively preventing another child from joining their play.

■ **guidance talk**

Used when one or two children have a conflict directly with an adult, such as when they skip out instead of cleaning up, or when they need additional teaching after a conflict is resolved (for example, after a child is hurt during a conflict).

■ **class meeting**

Used when children experience social conflicts that may impact the whole class—for example, when children begin calling each other "butthead" or use the climber in ways that might cause others to fall.

■ **comprehensive guidance**

Used when a child experiences serious mistaken behaviors that continue over time (such as repeated tantrums or withdrawing behavior).

There are many published models for social problem solving, ranging from as few as three steps to as many as 20 or more (Gartrell, 2003). While most models are designed for addressing conflicts directly between children, many can be adapted for use in any situation. I suggest an informal five-step problem-solving model of conflict management (Gartrell, 2000). I call it the "five-finger formula" because each step can be counted off on a finger.

1. **Cool down** (thumb). If necessary, the teacher calms down all parties (including herself or himself) and sets the scene for the mediation process. Note that the teacher may temporarily separate or remove children as part of this step—but only as a cooling-off period that leads to mediation, not as a punishment.

2. **Identify the problem** (pointer). The children (with help from the teacher as needed) put the problem into words and agree on what it is.

3. **Brainstorm solutions** (tall guy). The children (with the teacher's help as needed) come up with possible ways to solve the problem.

4. **Go for it** (ringer). The parties decide on one solution and try it. The teacher works for agreement on the solution, even if she or he must suggest it. Often, before a solution is implemented, the teacher has a guidance talk with the children, reviewing what happened, talking about alternatives for next time, and discussing ways to make amends.

5. **Follow-up** (pinky). The teacher follows up by encouraging, monitoring, and if necessary guiding the children as they try the solution. A guidance talk with one or more children may also be a part of this step.

With adaptations depending on the situation, the five-finger approach can be applied to all four types of conflict situations.

CLASSIC CONFLICT MANAGEMENT

When a conflict happens, under traditional discipline the typical teacher reaction is to comfort the "victim" and punish the "perpetrator." The previous chapter discusses the impact of punishment on the child causing the conflict. A child cannot be "shamed into being nice." The child learns no positive alternative behavior and is likely to internalize a mix of negative emotions that may make it even harder to "be nice" next time. If the teacher continues to view the child as "not nice," the danger of a negative self-fulfilling prophecy being ingrained becomes real.

It is important to note that the child who is victimized also suffers. He or she has little opportunity for justice beyond comforting by the authority figure and the occasional forced apology. Too often the victim stays a victim (in the child's own eyes and the eyes of others), vulnerable to future violence (Nansel et al., 2001). By failing to teach the victimized child to be rightfully assertive, traditional discipline may actually perpetuate, rather than reduce, bully-victim relationships.

Because conflict management is guidance, the teacher focuses on making both parties equal contributors to a peaceful settlement through mediation. (In *mediation,* a third party helps others settle a conflict; in *negotiation,* the parties resolve the conflict themselves.) During the mediation the teacher puts aside who is to blame and who is victimized (Carlsson-Paige & Levin, 2000) and encourages both parties to see themselves as full citizens of the classroom community, capable of solving their problems together and learning from their mistakes. Over time the teacher shares authority for the mediation with the children, gradually moving them to negotiate their conflicts on their own (Wichert, 1989). The teacher often ends or follows the mediation with a guidance talk, especially if harm was caused during the conflict.

After successful conflict mediation, in contrast to punitive interventions, teachers often see the children who were just arguing resume play together (Gartrell, 2003). Conflict management as a primary intervention technique helps create classrooms that are not just orderly, but encouraging and peaceable as well (Wichert, 1989). Classic conflict management is so key to moving beyond traditional discipline, including time-out, that it is the "featured technique" of this chapter.

The Technique at Work

The following anecdote about a preschool conflict illustrates conflict management at work. Vivian, a student teacher, attempted for the first time to mediate a classroom conflict.

During my observation, I watched and listened to two children arguing about how much time each could spend using a keyboard and earphones in the music center. Ennis said he was upset with Callie because she was taking too long in the area. He said she had forgotten to set the timer for 10 minutes and had been there a lot longer.

Callie: I set the timer. Look at it if you don't believe me.

Ennis: You just set it a few minutes ago when I asked you how much time!

Callie: I'm staying until the time is up.

Next, Ennis hit Callie on the back. Then Callie kicked at Ennis from her chair and her earphones fell around her neck.

I had stayed close, but not too close during the entire argument, hoping that maybe the children would be able to work out their problem. Now I went over, asked them both to sit on chairs, and helped them calm down. I asked Ennis what happened. He told me his version of the events I had observed. I responded, "That is a problem, but I can't let you hit other students, and I won't let them hit you. Let's hear what Callie has to say." She told me her side.

I told Callie she should set the timer before she starts playing the keyboard so that she doesn't forget, because other children do not want to be left out. I asked both children, "How can we fix this so you don't fight?" The two children seemed too bummed-out to respond, so I suggested, "How about if Callie sets the timer for 5 minutes to finish up, and then Ennis can set the timer for the full 10 minutes?" They agreed, and I reminded them that next time they should remember to set the timer at the start of their turns. A few minutes later the timer rang and I observed Callie give the earphones to Ennis. (Gartrell, 2000)

The dispute between Ennis and Callie was about privilege—who has the privilege of using the keyboard for how long. (The issue of when privilege is fair and when it is not is a common source of conflicts in early childhood classrooms.) Vivian used high-level mediation here—that is, she felt the children needed her direct leadership to solve the problem. She knew that when teachers try to mediate conflicts, they don't have to do it perfectly. Let us explore how she used the five steps of conflict management at the high (active coaching) mediation level:

1. **Cool down.** Vivian has both children sit down before beginning the mediation. She doesn't need to remove them from the situation, but sees they need help cooling down before they can talk.

2. **Identify the problem.** Vivian hears both children's versions of what happened. They both pretty much agree what the problem is and don't dispute Vivian's restatement. The agreement is apparent later when they also agree on a solution. At this second step, Vivian has

Learning from Vivian's Experience

- Vivian does not intervene right away. Da Ros and Kovach (1998) point out that adults frequently intervene too quickly, even with toddlers. Although it takes fortitude, adults sometimes wait until minor hitting occurs, which is what Vivian does here. With a real threat of physical harm, however, it is important to act quickly to de-escalate the situation.

- When one or more children lose emotional control, conflict management is still necessary. But people cannot talk through a problem when they are upset! This is why the first step is so important. Even the teacher may need a moment to calm down. Once in control of her own emotions, the teacher separates the children, helps them cool down, and mediates.

- Vivian does not take the keyboard away from the children, a common reaction under traditional discipline. Instead of making loss of the keyboard a punishment, she makes access a part of the curriculum, using it to teach the children democratic life skills.

- She does not force an apology. When people are expected to apologize before they are ready to, they usually carry unresolved negative feelings, which may come out later. Successful conflict management increases the chances of authentic reconciliation.

- Vivian might have used the guidance talk at the end of the process rather during step two. However, teachers do not have to follow the steps to the letter for mediation to basically succeed. (Certainly, children's own efforts at negotiation may not be by the book.) The proof of the carrot cake is in the eating. Vivian's first try at conflict mediation is a success—as first mediation efforts of most of my students are—and a gnarly old professor cannot ask for more than this.

a brief guidance talk about their behavior. Teachers often wait until the conflict is mediated to have this talk. Before a conflict is resolved, feelings of guilt can inhibit reaching a solution—which may have happened here.

3. **Brainstorm solutions.** Vivian invites the children to give ideas for "how to fix this so you don't fight." One reason she uses high-level mediation is that the children seem "bummed out" and are not ready to suggest solutions.

4. **Go for it.** Vivian suggests a solution that the children agree to. A key difference between conflict mediation and traditional discipline is that the teacher does not force a solution. If the children don't accept a solution, the teacher goes back to step three. Children often come up with a different solution from the "ideal" one the teacher has in mind. Teachers should try to use the children's ideas, even when they believe justice is not completely served. If the children work it out and agree to it, the solution is logical to them and they benefit from the process. The end of step four is the preferred place for a guidance talk (not step two), occasionally including follow-up with one or both children later.

5. **Follow-up.** Vivian observes the children put the solution into practice. As mentioned, the relief of successfully resolving a dispute sometimes brings the children back together in the activity. But any mediator would settle for the peaceful exchange of the keyboard when the timer rings—with no further need for adult intervention. When following up with a guidance talk, a teacher might start with encouragement of how the children implemented the solution peaceably (Gartrell, 2000).

GUIDANCE TALKS

Guidance talks between a teacher and child occur either during or after the last steps in conflict management or, when appropriate, instead of conflict management. Some conflicts are directly between a child and a teacher, especially over program expectations such as using equipment safely, starting an activity, or resting. The guidance talk, held privately to avoid embarrassment, differs from the age-old lecture. Instead of an adult talking *at* a child, the guidance talk is a conversation *with* the child. Its purpose is to teach the child that he or she can respond differently in conflict situations and to coach the child on specific alternatives.

In holding a guidance talk, the teacher:

■ discusses what happened and conveys an understanding about why the behavior was mistaken. For example, she helps the child understand it is okay to feel frustrated when the top of the glue bottle comes off with the glue, but it is not all right to throw the bottle and accidentally hit a friend.

- helps the child understand how all parties in the situation may have felt. (A goal of guidance talks is to build empathy.)

- brainstorms with the child alternative acceptable behaviors to use the next time a similar situation arises. "Next time, you can say, 'That makes me angry!' Or come to me and say, 'Teacher, help!' And I will."

- asks how the child can help the other child feel better or how the situation can be made better. (Note, this is different from forcing an apology. Neither children nor adults benefit when they are pressured to "say you're sorry" before the issues and feelings around them are resolved. When children are helped to resolve the conflict and invited to participate in the reconciliation, they are usually much more able than adults to forgive and forget.) If the teacher and child can't think of a way to make amends, the teacher can suggest that the child think about it and come up with an idea later. Children usually do come up with their own ideas for getting back together. Friendly relations are important to young children—they just have to get over the conflict first.

Self-Removal

As a result of guidance talks and growing trust between child and teacher, a strategy for "next time" might be self-removal by the child (Marion, 1999). Teachers need to work closely with the child and classmates so self-removal does not have the stigma of punishment. (One teacher set up an attractive "peace island" in a corner of the classroom. She tells the children that whenever they need to get away, they can travel to the island. The teachers watch for island visitors and offer their assistance as appropriate.) Occasionally even a teacher visits the island.

Common reasons that a child removes himself or herself from a situation are to work through an impulse or regain emotional control (Marion, 1999). As such, self-removal is often a targeted response used with some children rather than a more general problem-solving approach. Just as conflict management follows a cooling-down time, self-removal is usually followed by a guidance talk. An effective form of self-removal is for the child to voluntarily leave a situation and approach the teacher for assistance. Self-removal is not the final step in a child's learning to manage emotions. But for children who need it, self-removal is an important step.

CLASS MEETINGS

Some readers may remember group punishments from their own school experiences. Perhaps everyone had to put their heads down on their desks or stay in at recess because a few children were aggressive on the playground or too loud in the hall. The guidance alternative to group punishments is the class meeting, which uses the five steps of social problem solving, formally or informally, to resolve the situation (Gartrell, 2003).

Some teachers hold class meetings once or twice a week, others two or even three times a day (Harris & Fuqua, 2000; McClurg 1998). The frequency depends on whether the meetings are used to discuss routine business in addition to problems that affect the class. Here are common guidelines for classroom meetings:

- One person speaks at a time.
- Everyone listens carefully and respects others' views.
- Everyone appreciates all members of the class.

While the teacher remains the leader during class meetings, many teachers share leadership with the children as the year goes on. Unlike group punishments, regular meetings make classrooms more democratic and encouraging.

Two former students sent me anecdotes of class meetings held to address a common problem: too much commotion while walking down the hall. In each case a preschool classroom was located at the end of a wing of an elementary school. Teachers in classrooms of older students complained to the principal about the noise made by the preschoolers when walking down the hall. Recognizing that young children and line-travel are not a natural match, each teacher discussed the problem with her class, asked for solutions, decided on one, and successfully tried it (Gartrell, 2003).

In one case the children decided to be quiet mice, tiptoeing in the hall so the cat wouldn't hear them. In the other the children decided to be mother and father elephants, walking quietly so as not to wake up the babies. In this second situation, the principal came out of his office and loudly complimented the children on how quietly they were walking. "Shh," said one child, "you'll wake the babies!" These examples show that when teachers work with children to solve problems, rather than impose solutions on them, class meetings can contribute to a positive spirit of community.

COMPREHENSIVE GUIDANCE

Serious mistaken behavior is the result of strong unmet emotional and/or physical needs that the child cannot cope with or understand (Curry & Arnaud, 1995; Gartrell, 1995; Heath, 1994). When a teacher encounters a child whose unmet needs result in extreme and repeated mistaken behavior, guidance is both vital and difficult to use. When working with children who show serious mistaken behavior, the following considerations are important:

- **There is no such thing as a bad child.** There are children with serious problems who need our help so they can solve them.

- **Children showing serious mistaken behavior often are the hardest children to like.** Nevertheless, they are probably most in need of a helping relationship with a caring adult.

- **Children may show serious mistaken behavior in the classroom because it is the safest place in their lives.** They are asking for help with their problems in the only way they can, even by using mistaken behavior.

- **The more serious the mistaken behavior, the more comprehensive the approach needed and the more people a teacher may need.** It is especially important to involve the family in helping the child learn to use alternative behaviors to meet his or her needs. Other staff and outside professionals may also need to be added to the team.

- **Children who show repeated aggressive and extreme behaviors are in danger of being stigmatized by peers and adults.** Stigma means disqualification from full membership in the group (Gartrell, 2003). Ladd (1989) and Nansel and colleagues (2001) point out that an internalized pattern of rejection in childhood can cause lifelong social and emotional difficulties.

- **Teachers can reach out to children at risk for stigma and help them turn around their lives by building positive attachments with them, assisting them to find membership in the class, and teaching them democratic life skills.** Such teaching, termed *liberation teaching,* is at the heart of what guidance is about (Gartrell, 2003). (See further Chapter 9.)

Generally, children respond positively when teachers build relationships with them and their families and create and maintain encouraging classrooms. But children with strong unmet needs may be too burdened to respond to everyday guidance practices. For example, in a case study in Chapter 5, Jamal was showing stress from transition to and from foster care when he hit a classmate. After unsuccessful use of time-out, the teacher took several therapeutic actions that together helped the child. Children like Jamal, facing tough life circumstances, need comprehensive guidance that includes most or all of the following steps:

- **encouragement to build healthy attachments** with one or more staff. The person who builds this special relationship is often the lead teacher or another adult who gets along well with the child (Rich, 1993). On occasion the person may be a specialist

(Sang, 1994). Jamal's teacher made personal time for him each morning, and this made a difference. A child must feel fully accepted before he can dare to change.

■ **assistance in situations that may lead to loss of control,** before conflicts occur. For instance, a teacher might help a child recognize when she feels tense and encourage her to ask for assistance and/or use self-removal to leave a situation.

■ **firm, friendly, consistent intervention** that may involve accompanied removal to cool down but always includes conflict mediation and/or a guidance talk (Marion, 1999). This crisis intervention helps children understand what happened and how all parties are feeling; what they can do instead next time; and how they can make the other parties feel better (not through a forced apology). Guided self removal often may be part of the follow-up strategy.

■ **meetings of staff, and of staff with families,** using the five steps of social problem solving to set a coordinated course of action (sometimes called an Individual Guidance Plan). The IGP outlines a coordinated, agreed to strategy that staff and family (to the extent possible) follow. The IGP addresses each of the bulleted points, and sets a timeline for periodic review.

■ **inclusion of other adults in the comprehensive plan** as needed. First and foremost, teachers need to involve families. The time to begin building relationships, of course, is at the start of the program or school year—not at the time of crisis. If additional adults are needed, teachers and families ask special education teachers, mental health consultants, senior staff members, or others to observe and become involved. As professionals, teachers collaborate to accomplish together what they cannot accomplish alone (Gartrell, 2003).

TEACHERS NEED SUPPORT, TOO

As a final note, for teachers to use guidance effectively, they must have their own support systems. In the classroom, they create a teaching team—adults with differing backgrounds and educational credentials who work together for the good of all members of the classroom community. The adults build a mutually supportive teaching team so all know they can rely on each other when children have crises or long-term needs.

Teachers also build partnerships with families, beginning at the start of the program or school year. The problem-solving process works more effectively when a teacher knows a family well. The research is compelling that children are more likely to succeed at school when families and teachers work together (Coleman, 1997; DeJong & Cottrell, 1999;

Gorham & Nason, 1997). As volunteers, family members of course may also be part of the teaching team.

Outside of the classroom, effective teachers seek positive personal connections with family, friends, and community. Teachers recognize the need for a measure of personal success—including financial security—so they can fully function as professionals in assisting children and families to learn and develop. This understanding is the first and last step in successfully using guidance and being a liberating teacher. It is a reality that the world outside of the early childhood community needs to better understand.

End Note: *The preceding chapter appeared in the March 2002 issue of* Young Children *under the original title: "Replacing Time-Out: Part Two—Using guidance to maintain an encouraging classroom. Gartrell, D. J. (2002).* Young Children, *(57) 2, 36–43.*

REFERENCES

Carlsson-Paige, N., & Levin, D. E. (2000). *Before push comes to shove: Building conflict resolution skills with children.* St. Paul, MN: Redleaf Press.

Coleman, M. (1997). Families and schools: In search of common ground. *Young Children, 52* (5), 14–21.

Curry, N. E., & Arnaud, S. H. (1995). Personality difficulties in preschool children as revealed through play themes and styles. *Young Children, 50* (4), 4–9.

Da Ros, D. A., & Kovach, B. A. (1998). Assisting toddlers and caregivers during conflict resolutions: Interactions that promote socialization. *Childhood Education, 75* (1), 25–30.

DeJong, L., & Cottrell, B. H. (1999). Designing infant child care programs to meet the needs of children born to teenage parents. *Young Children, 54* (1), 37–45.

Gartrell, D. J. (1995). Misbehavior or mistaken behavior? *Young Children, 50* (5), 27–34.

Gartrell, D. J. (2003). *A guidance approach for the encouraging classroom* (3rd ed.). Clifton Park, NY: Delmar Learning.

Gartrell, D. J. (2000). *What the kids said today: Using classroom conversations to become a better teacher.* St. Paul, MN: Redleaf Press.

Gartrell, D. J. (2001). Replacing time-out: Part one—Using guidance to build an encouraging classroom. *Young Children, 56* (6), 8–16.

Gorham, P. J., & Nason, P. N. (1997). Why make teachers' work more visible to parents? *Young Children, 52* (5), 22–26.

Harris, T. T., & Fuqua, J. D. (2000). What goes around comes around: Building a community of learners through circle times. *Young Children, 55* (1), 44–47.

Heath, H. E. (1994). Dealing with difficult behaviors—Teachers plan with parents. *Young Children, 49* (5), 20–24.

Ladd, G. W. (1989, April). *Children's friendships in the classroom: Precursors of early school adaptation*. Paper presented at the biennial meeting of the Society for Research in Child Development, Kansas City, MO.

Marion, M. (1999). *Guidance of young children*. New York: Merrill.

McClurg, L. G. (1998). Building an ethical community in the classroom: Community meeting. *Young Children, 53* (2), 30–35.

Nansel, T. R., Overpeck, M., Pilla, R. S., Ruan, W. J., Simons-Morton, B., & Scheidt, P. (2001). Bullying behaviors among U.S. youth: Prevalence and association with psychosocial adjustment. *Journal of the American Medical Association, 285* (16), 2094–2100.

Rich, B. A. (1993). Listening to Harry (and solving a problem) in my kindergarten classroom. *Young Children, 48* (6), 52.

Sang, D. (1994). The worry teacher comes on Thursdays. *Young Children, 49* (2), 24–31.

Schreiber, M. E. (1999). Time-outs for toddlers: Is our goal punishment or education? *Young Children, 54* (4), 22–25.

Wichert, S. (1989). *Keeping the peace*. Philadelphia: New Society.

CHAPTER 7

Sustaining the Encouraging Classroom: Class Meetings

QUICK TAKE

Chapter 7 continues the discussion of class meetings, begun in the last chapter. As a primary method for modeling citizenship in a democracy, class meetings are central to teaching democratic life skills. Meetings are a primary vehicle for making these skills part of the curriculum. Class meetings teach and review the guidelines necessary to keep classrooms encouraging. Regular meetings establish that the classroom is not just the teacher's domain, with children as long-term guests, but a place belonging to all, with all having the right to learn. The meetings foster a sense of ownership in, and responsibility for, the encouraging classroom.

Within the realm of guidance, class meetings extend social problem solving into the public domain. When problems of name-calling or peer-exclusion or widespread neglect of guidelines occur, the teacher and children use class meetings to solve the problem together. In this respect, the class meeting is the guidance alternative to the traditional group punishment—"Everyone put your heads down on your desks and think about how you were noisy." Or, "Everyone lie down on your mats and think about how we walk in line." You get the idea. A contrasting expression at a class meeting is, "Some of us had a problem today when we were in line. Let's talk about the problem and figure out how to solve it."

Chapter 7 offers guidance for making class meetings a regular part of the education program, even for preschoolers, and discusses further the benefits outlined here.

Circle gatherings long have been used by Native Americans and other cultural groups for public deliberation in a spirit of equality. Circle times in the classroom go back at least to Froebel's first kindergartens in Germany in the 1840s. For Froebel, the circle represented the non-beginning/ non-ending of the universe and the unity of humankind with God. Whether or not modern teachers work from this symbolism, the circle suggests the equality and worth of each individual and lends itself to the community spirit that is the objective of the class meeting.

In classrooms today, the term *circle time* refers to a large-group gathering with children seated on the floor that typically focuses on daily routines and educational activities. Though the specifics differ across classrooms, circle times often include a combination of the following activities: attendance, weather, calendar, lunch count, finger plays, songs, stories, and lead-in for the day's academic program. As Harris and Fuqua (2000) suggest, when teachers keep circle times concise and engaging, children are more likely to be attentive participants.

A circle formation is also common to class meetings, and on occasion circle times flow into class meetings (Vance & Weaver, 2002). But, class meetings have a different focus, transcending daily routines to deal with life in the classroom. Class meetings encourage reflection and sharing by children and teachers about their experiences, needs, concerns, problems, and triumphs. About the "community" meeting (McClurg's term for the class meeting)—McClurg says:

> The purpose of the community meeting is to create an intentional community devoted to a common project: learning to live with and take in the realities and perspectives of others. Here young children encounter and learn to acknowledge multiple realities, discover that they have choices, and realize that they are responsible for their decisions, (1998, pp. 30–31).

Teachers choose to hold class meetings in order to establish a sense of belonging within the group, conduct class business, and to solve problems that arise. Whatever the immediate purpose, guidelines such as the following apply:

- Anyone can talk.
- Take turns and listen carefully.
- Be honest.
- Be kind.

Developing these guidelines, and the reasons for them, may well be the subject of early class meetings (Castle & Rogers, 1993/1994). Guidelines—statements of "do's"—frame the standards of conduct for the encouraging classroom. In contrast, rules tend to be stated in the negative—"Don't talk when some else is." Rules tend to make teachers and children think of the classroom in terms of conformity, defiance, and enforcement. Because the intent of guidelines is to teach rather than induce obedience, established guidelines in activities like class meetings are the "constitution" of the encouraging classroom (Gartrell, 2003). During the first class meetings, teachers use the creation of guidelines (through consensus rather than "voting") to engender a spirit of community within the class.

In addition to guidelines for the class, the teacher might also have personal guidelines for class meetings:

- Support each child in the expression of his or her views.
- Maintain a positive, caring focus.
- Personal situations may require private remedies.
- Meetings are to solve problems, not create them.
- Build an encouraging community that includes everyone.

McClurg points out that meetings teach the group living skills that adults generally want all children to learn:

> Some children may be too self-conscious; others may need to become more self-aware. Some may need to take control, while others are learning how to give. It is good news that, with a little leadership from an understanding adult, young children can learn these and many other things from each other. (1998, p. 30)

Class meetings, then, become a primary method for teaching democratic life skills. Each time a meeting occurs, children are reminded the classroom is a community that includes everyone, both children and adults (Greenberg, 1992). Just as learning centers do, class meetings help to define the encouraging classroom.

Anecdote

A prekindergarten teacher held a class meeting before playtime. Marcie explained to the class that there were some problems happening on the climber and asked if some children could share about them.

One child said, "I got bumped on the top and I nearly falled off."

Another child said, "Somebody stepped on my fingers when I was climbing up."

A third child complained, "I was going down the slide and someone was comin up and I bumped him."

Marcie helped the children define the problem a bit more. Then she asked, "How can we solve this problem so no one gets hurt and we can use the climber safely?"

She wrote down the children's ideas, stating them positively, as guidelines:

1. We sit or crawl on the top and don't stand.

2. We give other people room, like when they are climbing up.

3. We go down the slide, except on Fridays. (Marcie really liked this one because she was wanting them to get more upper-body exercise. Also, the practice seemed to increase the children's calendar awareness about Fridays.)

Marcie slowly read the guidelines back to the children. She "ceremoniously" posted them by the climber. For a few days, she or another adult stayed close to the climber and provided reminders about the guidelines. By that time, the children had all memorized them and reminded each other.

CLASSROOM MEETINGS/MAGIC CIRCLES

William Glasser is credited with popularizing the use of class meetings (1969), sometimes also called "magic circles." In Glasser's model, class meetings are held to identify problems and work toward solutions. The meetings center around behavior issues, curriculum matters, or student concerns. Glasser is adamant that the class meeting occurs without blame or fault finding. Honest opinions stated and respected are the keys that make the method work. When children know they have a say in how the program goes and how it can be made better, they feel like they belong and want to contribute.

In a 1989 account of the writing of Glasser on building "a sense of togetherness" within the class, Charles states:

To foster a sense of togetherness, the teacher should continually talk with the class about what they will accomplish *as a group,* how they will deal with the problems they encounter as a group, how they will work together to get the best achievement possible for every individual in the group. In order to bring this about, responsibilities are given and shared, students are encouraged to speak of their concerns while the class attempts to find remedies, and the teacher takes special steps, when necessary to incorporate every student into the ongoing work of the class. (p. 142)

Wolfgang (1999) points out that in Glasser's classroom meetings, there are no wrong answers; every child can successfully participate without fear of correction. The teacher works for this goal with direct teaching about the meeting process, but also with ongoing verbal and nonverbal support. To reduce her own personal judgments during meetings, the teacher might use *reflective statements* that affirm what a child has said or meant:

Child: "Den the snow wented down my back! Brrrr."

Teacher: "The snow went down your back? You must have felt very cold!"

The teachers also may use nondirective statements:

Child: "I could write it in a story, but I don't know how to."

Teacher: "Well, you think about how you want to do it and let me know if you come up with an idea."

Just as much as supportive comments, the teacher relies on the staple nonverbal responses of *nods and smiles,* allowing the children as much as possible to guide the discussion's flow (Wolfgang, 1999).

For Glasser, there were three types of classroom meetings: open ended, educational/diagnostic, and problem solving (Wolfgang, 1999). The **open-ended meeting** discusses hypothetical life problems—"What if you saw a child had left a quarter on her desk. What would you do?" (When young children share personal experiences with the group, teachers can sometimes guide discussions into this type of meeting.)

The second type, the **educational/diagnostic meeting,** is for the purpose of conversing about educational ideas—such as the topic of missing teeth when a dentist is coming to visit—as part of a project on "our teeth." Vance and Weaver (2002) emphasize the compatibility of class meetings with the project method, for planning, sharing, evaluating, and celebrating project activities. The authors state:

Project work is a beneficial but challenging teaching strategy, and class meetings can address these challenges through increased communication. When teachers share the planning of project work with the class, children feel ownership in the way projects develop (p. 56).

The third type, the **problem-solving meeting,** is for the purpose of discussing real conflicts occurring in the classroom. For instance, holding a class meeting with preschoolers when play outside has gotten too rambunctious. Discussion about this third type of class meeting, integral to the guidance approach, continues under another heading.

Holding Class Meetings

Writers have different ideas about how often to hold class meetings. Mc-Clurg suggests a weekly meeting of at least a half-hour for a first-grade class (1998). In contrast, also at a kindergarten/first-grade level, Harris and Fuqua recommend three meetings a day. Harris and Fuqua (2000) state: "Twenty minutes, three times a day spent in building a sense of community, we predict, will have an impact on all aspects of the day and make all other times more productive with less time spent in overt management" (p. 47).

Because they are central to the encouraging classroom, I recommend two scheduled meetings a day both at the prekindergarten and primary-grade level—after arrival (and breakfast when possible) and just before going home. The teacher can also call special meetings if something eventful happens that needs immediate discussion.

The morning meeting might follow a concise, interactive circle time. A segue might be special events, reported by any child, such as a new pet or a visit to the doctor's. The teacher too might contribute a topic at this time, perhaps one that ties in with a project, theme, or content area. She must take care, however, to share the discussion with the children, for the essence of the class meeting is a sharing of authority with the class (Harris & Fuqua, 2000; McClurg, 1998). (This is where the democracy comes in.) With knowledge of the group, such discussions are not difficult to spark. At a morning class meeting, before a dentist (the mother of one of the children) was to visit, a first-grade teacher asked: "I wonder. Have you or someone that you know ever had a tooth come out?"

Teachers should handle special event discussions with sensitivity for another reason. Some experiences, such as a hospital stay or death of someone close to a child, may be painful to discuss. Whenever possible, the teacher should know the children and their families well enough to discuss such matters privately first. (Some experiences are best kept private.) We cannot always know everything beforehand, of course. Sometimes young children do share the "darndest" things; this comes with the territory:

> In my kindergarten I had a little boy named Dean who was very shy. One day in group he raised his hand and quietly mumbled,

"I had to wear these shoes today because I got b'ture on my good ones."

I asked him what he had said. He again mumbled it. I said, "You got what?" He looked with frustration at me and said loud and clear, "Cow shit!"

(Sometimes a teacher has to accentuate the positive, especially when you've put your foot in it yourself.) "Oh, Dean, now I know what you said! You got cow manure on your shoe. That's not much fun, is it?"

One widespread phobia in the United States is a fear of public speaking. When a child speaks up in a class meeting, as in any group situation, we need to be inclusive of his comments—even when they are embarrassing—so he still feels part of the group and not separated from it. Anyway, who has not gotten manure of one kind or another on his shoe? (Gartrell, 2000)

A second time for holding scheduled class meetings is just before going home. The purposes of the meeting are to review the day and discuss coming events. As well, group members might share something they learned or enjoyed doing, or something that did not go well. For instance, the teacher or a child might bring up a learning center that was left messy or an accomplishment, like creating a mural, that someone is pleased with.

When a teacher or child experiences a problem, the end of the day meeting is a time to discuss it (Greenberg, 1992; Harris & Fuqua, 2000).

If an afternoon meeting becomes too involved though, the teacher asks the class to think about the issue overnight so that "we can discuss it in the morning when we are fresh." The teacher works to end the meeting on a positive note. The teacher may acknowledge a student who shared in a notable way, sing a song with the children, or ask for a volunteer to share how they solved a problem on their own (Vance & Weaver, 2002).

Vance and Weaver (2002) offer helpful advice for teachers ready to try class meetings with their children:

> If you are just beginning to use class meetings and are weighing the benefits, make a commitment to hold them for at least three months before judging the results. It may take that long for children to incorporate their new social skills, begin to use them regularly, and learn to trust one another. The change in the classroom's social climate will be noticeable. (pp. 24–25)

Meeting to Solve Problems

A vital use of the class meeting is to resolve conflicts that affect the group (public, often Level Two, mistaken behaviors). In a previous section, we saw how a teacher used a class meeting to remind her preschoolers about safety on a climber. Other examples include when a daily routine repeatedly gets out of hand, or a word like "butt head" is catching on and driving the adults in the room "bananas." Class meetings to solve problems may occur during regular morning or afternoon time slots. But sometimes, the teacher calls unscheduled class meetings if a problem becomes urgent—a pressing teachable moment.

According to Glasser (1969), the teacher models the following discussion skills in all class meetings, but especially those called to solve problems:

1. The dignity of individuals is protected.
2. Situations are described, not judged.
3. Feelings are stated as I messages.
4. Suggestions for solutions are appreciated.
5. A course of action is decided, tried, and reviewed.

Class meetings that focus on problems provide an excellent opportunity for learning, gaining empathy and problem-solving abilities. Some of the most important learning that the class and teachers will do occurs during class meetings:

> In Vicki's kindergarten class, Gary wet his pants. A volunteer took Gary to the nurse's office where extra clothes were kept. Vicki overheard some of the children talking about Gary and decided it was time for an unscheduled class meeting. She explained to them what had happened. She told them a story about when she was a little girl, she wet her pants too and felt very embarrassed. Vicki told the class that people sometimes have accidents, even adults, and it is important that we be friendly so they don't feel badly. Vicki then paused and waited for a response.
>
> The children began to share similar experiences they remembered. When Gary came back to the room, another child smiled at him and said, "It's OK, Gary. Last time I wet my pants too."
>
> Other children added, "Me too." Looking greatly relieved, Gary took his seat. The class got back to the activities of the day.

Class Meetings and Level Three Mistaken Behaviors

A particularly difficult problem that every teacher faces is whether and how to explain to the rest of the class serious mistaken behaviors that one child shows. The teacher must balance the right of the child for the dignity of privacy with the need for other children to express their feelings about the behavior and to try to understand (Vance & Weaver, 2002). There is no magic answer to this dilemma. In a course journal once, a teacher shared that she felt she had no alternative but to "go public" when a child over time had many and violent conflicts in her first-grade class. Here is her account, slightly adapted:

OBSERVATION

One day, after Toby calmed down from a tantrum, I told him that we had to have a class meeting and called the children together. After seating Toby beside me, I explained to him and the class that he had been hurting others and himself for days, and he needed to hear from the other children how that made them feel. With the mutual respect I had been stressing, each child told Toby how his actions made them feel sad, mad, or scared. When one child said, "I want to be your friend, but I'm scared 'cause you hit me," Toby hung his head and whispered he was sorry.

I thanked the class and told them that Toby was trying hard to use his words and be friendly and that maybe the other boys and girls could help him. I stayed close to Toby the rest of the day, and helped him into class activities. Outside of class I worked with the parents and the special education teacher to get Toby additional assistance. Whereas before, most class members were actively avoiding Toby, some now sought to include him—warily to be sure, but they tried. Toby's struggles became less, but I am still not completely sure I did the right thing.

"Going public" about conflicts concerning an individual child is a difficult choice, though both Glasser (1969) and Vance and Weaver (2002) make the case that this is a valid use of class meetings. Teachers who do so open themselves and their children to fairly complex social dynamics. At any point the teacher must be prepared to step in to retain a spirit of mutual respect. The following anecdote was recorded by Marta, a student teacher in a rural, multicultural primary-grade classroom. Upon graduation, Marta received a contract from the school, which she accepted.

Anecdote

One of the children that we'll call Chris exhibited mistaken behavior on a regular basis. He did things like tipping over his desk, laying on the floor, getting up from his desk on impulse, and other types of mistaken behavior. On this day, Chris started out on the wrong foot, and things grew progressively worse as the day wore on. Right before lunch, after a series of crises, I ended up asking his special education teacher to work with Chris in her office out of the classroom.

I knew the children were bothered by what they had seen. After lunch, I held an unscheduled class meeting. I started out by saying "Sometimes when we come to school, we don't feel good about something that is going on at our home or with our friends. Many of us go to our parents or to someone we trust and talk about how we feel. Sometimes when we haven't been able to let our feelings come out, they start to sneak out in ways that maybe we don't want them to. I think that is how Chris is feeling today. I think he has some feelings that he needs to get out because they are starting to sneak out in ways he can't help. Before lunch today, Mrs. O. helped Chris down to her office so that she could maybe help him get rid of some of those scary feelings."

One child raised a hand and said, "Yea, one time I was so mad at Joe I could have hit him, but I went home and talked to my Mom and that helped."

Another child says, "So you mean that Chris doesn't tip his desk over on purpose?"

I said, "Yes, that is what I mean."

Another student raised their hand and said, "But sometimes I get mad and I don't tip my desk."

Her neighbor said, "Maybe you aren't mad like Chris."

We had just finished an Ojibwe story about a boy and a butterfly. The story was an analogy about people and their feelings. The last comment made was by one of the girls and she said, "Chris is like the butterfly with the broken wing."

It was so sweet I could have cried. I said, "Yes, Chris has a broken wing." We ended the class meeting and I felt like the children had a better understanding of their classmate.

REFLECTION

I can honestly say I have learned a great deal each time I had to deal with a problem, not only about solving problems, but about kids as well. I think the biggest thing I learned here was how effective a class meeting can be at helping children understand their classmates. The class meeting allowed them to really think about how Chris felt. I saw this when a child related his story of being so angry that he wanted to hit Joe. By discussing this they had a better understanding of Chris. I also felt they needed to know that Chris was not out there tipping his desk over for the fun of it. Deep down inside, Chris is a hurt little boy trying to cope with a problem that is bigger than he is. I wanted the class to try to see that in him. When Luella made that reference to the butterfly, I knew I had succeeded in that area.

Another thing that I learned was how effective a class meeting can be at solving a class problem that could have gotten worse. If we didn't have that talk, maybe some of the kids would have teased Chris when he came back into the room. Instead they treated him with respect. I was very pleased to see this response when he did return. Chris did continue with his mistaken behavior during the remainder of the day, but the kids ignored it. They seemed to understand that Chris was having a bad day and needed his space. (Gartrell, 2000)

A basic guidance principle is that to avoid embarrassment, a teacher tries to keep her interventions with a child private. Real life, however, means the teacher must balance this principle with the right of the class to a sense of well-being. In this anecdote, and the previous as well, the teachers worked hard to preserve the dignity of the child, in his own eyes and in the eyes of the group. Notice that when involved in such a situation, children accustomed to the class meetings do respond. Through these meetings, the community of the encouraging classroom is sustained, and the learning of democratic life skills occurs.

Class Meetings at Different Age Levels?

To reiterate a point, class meetings are not necessarily more suited to the elementary than preschool age levels. Hendrick (1992) discusses using class meetings to teach "the principles of democracy in the early years." She comments that class meetings can be invaluable in "learning to trust in a group." Hendrick agrees with me that, "Even four-year-olds can participate successfully in making simple group decisions that solve social problems" (p. 52). She goes on to say:

Together, for example, they might plan ways to stop children from running through the room. They might also discuss which special outside activities to do. As children move on to kindergarten and first grade, opportunities of greater magnitude arise. (pp. 52–53)

In fact, class meetings—though not necessarily under this name—can happen even with toddlers. One of my favorite anecdotes is about a toddler room where biting had become a serious problem. Starting with a group meeting, the teachers taught these very young children this strategy: When a child approached in a menacing manner, they were to hold out their arm with hand up, and state firmly "Stop" or "No!" The teachers and children practiced together, and some children began to use it.

The teachers found that this response broke the impulse of the approaching child, alerted the teachers to get over to the situation for some quick problem solving, and helped children who might otherwise be victims to be rightfully assertive. With this strategy and accompanying guidance for all parties concerned (especially the children doing the biting) the problem lessened, to the relief of all. This fact was brought up in later meetings with the toddlers.

THE VALUE OF CLASS MEETINGS

As class meetings become established in the encouraging classroom, children come to value them. The teacher will know that community meetings are having an impact when children take more responsibility for running them, and the teacher is sometimes able to sit back and watch (McClurg, 1998).

> Over time, children will begin to care for one another, solve their own problems, feel more empowered and more in control of their learning, and come to view all in the community as their "teachers." It will be time well spent when the teacher sees what happens during [class meetings] coming around again and again. (Harris & Fuqua, 2000 p. 47).

During a workshop a teacher from a small high school once shared this story: The daughter of the superintendent, in the teacher's social studies class, had her bike thrown in a creek by some classmates. The student, who tried hard to get along with everyone, asked the teacher if she could hold a private meeting with the class. The teacher was unsure about this prospect, but gave the student 10 minutes—a very long time to be pacing outside your own classroom. (She met the principal while she was in the hall and explained to him what was happening. His response: "Only 10 minutes, and stay close."—there still are small country high schools like this.)

At the end of the time, the student came out and with a slight smile, thanked the teacher, and said the meeting was over. Nothing more was mentioned about the incident—apparently nothing had to be—and the student reported no more problems with her classmates. Class meetings can be held successfully with preschoolers, elementary children, teenagers, and college students alike. At all levels such meetings are at the heart of the encouraging classroom.

End Note: *Adapted from Chapter 8, "Leadership Communication with the Group," in Gartrell, D. J. (2003).* A Guidance Approach for the Encouraging Classroom (3rd ed.). *Clifton Park, NY: Delmar Learning.*

REFERENCES

Castle, K., & Rogers, K. (1993/1994). Rule-creating in a constructivist classroom community. *Childhood Education, 70*(2), 74–80.

Charles, C. M. (1989). *Building classroom discipline.* New York: Longman.

Gartrell, D. J. (2000). *What the kids said today: Using classroom conversations to become a better teacher.* St. Paul, MN: Redleaf Press.

Gartrell, D. J. (2003). *A guidance approach for the encouraging classroom (3rd ed.).* Clifton Park, NY: Delmar Learning.

Glasser, W. (1969). *Schools without failure.* New York: Harper & Row.

Greenberg, P. (1992). How to institute some simple democratic practices pertaining to respect, rights, responsibilities in your classroom without losing your leadership position. *Young Children, 47*(5), 10–21.

Harris, T. T., & Fuqua, J. D. (2000). What goes around comes around: Building a community of learners through circle times. *Young Children, 55*(1), 44–47.

Hendrick, J. (1992). Where does it all begin? Teaching the principles of democracy in the early years. *Young Children, 47*(3), 51–53.

McClurg, L. G. (1998). Building an ethical community in the classroom: Community meeting. *Young Children, 53*(2), 30–35.

Vance, E., & Weaver, P. J. (2002). *Class meetings: Young children solving problems together.* Washington, DC: National Association for the Education of Young Children.

Wolfgang, C. H. (1999). *Solving discipline problems in the classroom.* New York: John Wiley & Sons.

Guidance with Boys in Early Childhood Classrooms

By Margaret King with Dan Gartrell

In a workshop once, Dan asked the early childhood teachers attending to think of the one child in their class that they found most challenging. He then asked how many of these children were boys and how many girls. Twenty-seven of the 31 attending (all of whom were women) indicated boys. Many teachers find boys and their behavior, well, challenging. To Margaret King (first author of the chapter) and myself, the matter is not just "the gender issue" of "women teachers versus young boys."

Rather, the main issue is that for reasons of development and temperament, many boys have difficulty fitting the traditional classroom expectations of many teachers—even when these teachers hold a lot of other expectations that are developmentally appropriate. The matter is one of attitudes and techniques and not just the obvious gender factor. True, some men teachers may have an "inside track" on how to improve the match of young boys and the educational program—just because they've "been there, done that." And certainly, we need men teachers as well as women teachers dedicated to young children—the chapter in fact ends on this topic. But women teachers as well as men can further their understanding about guidance with boys, and that is what Chapter 8 is about.

For authors and readers alike, precautions need to be taken when regarding material directed to either subgroup of children, boys or girls. There is a decided need to avoid gender stereotypes about the one group and neglect of legitimate needs of the other. In writing this chapter, Margaret and I attempted to keep three considerations in mind.

- First, many boys show little of the typical behaviors of some boys that bother some teachers. We all need to avoid the stereo-typed thinking that "boys are this way; girls are that way."

- Second, this chapter is really about making early childhood programs more develop-mentally appropriate for *all* children. Our thinking is that the program and interven-tion strategies discussed here fundamentally benefit both boys and girls. (For instance, for long-term health reasons, girls as well as boys may benefit from increased physical activity during the daily program.)

- Third, some teachers—we think many— enjoy working with both boys and girls who radiate a certain rambunctiousness and independence of spirit. We hope that readers will be not just "newly aware" but basically reinforced in their responses per-taining to the boisterous enthusiasm brought by some children into early child-hood classrooms.

"Active," "aggressive," "challenging," and "noncompliant" are words often used to describe young boys. Even the most competent teacher is sometimes challenged by the behaviors exhibited by boys. Many teachers find it difficult to distinguish problem behavior from "boy behavior" that is normal. Educators frequently describe boys as socially immature or developmentally young. In a recent study Pastor and Reuben (2002) found that boys too frequently are labeled ADD or ADHD.

Teachers often view boys who are energetic and active as difficult to manage. They seem to spend a lot of time engaged in "off-task behavior" looking for and finding "mischief." Their behaviors may not match the traditional view of a smoothly operated classroom. In some classrooms it may be one or two boys who experience difficulties, while in others it may be the majority of boys in the classroom.

A COMPOSITE CASE STUDY

Chapter 8 presents a "composite case study" of several classrooms and teachers who have met and positively addressed the *boy problem*. This term is a misnomer, of course, typically used by teachers who have become frustrated in their efforts to understand and manage the behavior of boys in their classes. The case study follows Juanita in her progress from a teacher-technician who endures the class she is dealt until her patience runs out, to a teacher-professional who commits herself to changes in the educational program and her own response styles. By developing this composite case study, we discuss how teachers, as guidance professionals, can bring caring leadership to their work with young boys in their classes.

The chapter concludes with a response to a recent study of NAEYC membership, *The Importance of Men Teachers and Why There Are So Few* (Nelson, 2002) and a comment about the role of men teachers in guidance.

The Setting "Before"

Ten of the 14 children in Juanita's class of three-, four-, and five-year-olds were boys. A group of boys (between seven and nine) were making the classroom difficult for the teacher to manage. Sometimes they worked individually. Other times they worked collectively. The boys would dump containers of small Legos®, unifix cubes, or small blocks when the teacher was not looking. Other times they would wrestle with each other during story time or during other group activities—sometimes escalating into serious conflicts. When asked about their behavior, they would say "for fun" and then they would giggle. Even though the adults did not think that it was funny, the boys seemed to enjoy their "mischief." There was no question: the overall pattern of "mischief" was becoming persistent and disrupting the flow of the classroom. Juanita found herself worrying about the effects of the frequent conflicts on the boys themselves, the rest of the class, her assistant, and herself.

Juanita needed help in figuring out what to do. For this teacher, the solution was not simple because her classroom was well organized with well-defined areas and well-planned activities based on her knowledge of children's developmental levels and interest. This was the first time in her five years of teaching that she had a class that she could not manage. After attending a workshop at a conference titled "Boys in the Classroom," Juanita began to recognize something she only half understood before: that the problem was not the boys themselves, it was the way she was teaching them. Juanita realized that she saw the boys in her class as less mature and more "rowdy" versions of the mature children in her class, mainly girls who easily followed directions.

From the workshop, Juanita applied the criteria of mistaken behavior to analyze the pattern of conflicts she was seeing. The "mischief" often began as Level One, Experimentation mistaken behavior. Boys would get overinvolved in a situation and the "experiment" would get out of control; or they would test the limits of situations to find out about the consequences. By taunting or teaming, the boys also got each other involved, so Juanita was seeing Level Two, Socially Influenced mistaken behavior as well. With one or two of the boys, the mistaken behavior was more serious Level Three, Strong-Needs mistaken behavior. Juanita knew these boys to have difficult lives outside of the classroom. Just as she needed to give these two guys all of the assistance they needed, she had to make the class a more safe and positive community for all.

Juanita decided that she needed to change her classroom. An overriding thought was whether or not the problems in her class were related to gender differences. In other words, she wondered if she were more responsive to the needs of the girls; therefore, creating an environment that was less boy-friendly. She decided that she would address her concerns by asking two questions to guide her process of change. The two questions were:

> How could she create a classroom that was more responsive to the needs of all the children, and especially the boys who were not integrated into the culture of the classroom?

> How could she more appropriately handle the mistaken behavior of all children, and specifically individual boys, who were experiencing the greatest difficulty in her classroom?

> The chapter now focuses on these questions.

BUILDING AN ENCOURAGING CLASSROOM FOR BOYS

Question: How can Juanita create a classroom culture that is more responsive to the needs of the children in her class, and especially the boys? To begin the process of creating a classroom more inclusive of the needs of boys, Juanita analyzed what was specifically happening in the classroom. The teacher needed to understand what was happening in order to begin implementing change.

Using anecdotal observations of selected situations, Juanita documented how children were spending their time as well as typical samples of off-task behavior. She made a series of two part write-ups. *Part one* was an objective description of exactly what she saw and heard (and on one occasion smelled) in the selected situations. For example: "Noah was lying on his side in the block area, stacking the small unit blocks. Julian came running by, going after a toy truck that had just become available. He tripped over Noah's leg and scraped his knee on the heater grate. With his other leg he started to kick at Julian, who was still lying down. I separated the children and explained to them what happened. Julian was crying pretty hard so I used reflective listening to calm him down. Then the three of us talked about what happened. I explained it was an accident."

In *part two,* Juanita recorded her personal attempts to understand the meaning of the observation within the context of her classroom. For example, "I saw that Julian thought he had been tripped and was more angry than hurt. I held him and explained what had happened, letting him know it was an accident and it was all right to cry about being hurt. After he calmed down, we went over to where Noah was holding his own leg and talked about it. By the end, I think both boys understood the situation as each resumed play.

Juanita used this two-part system to objectively separate her observations from her thoughts about the observations, so minimizing quick and judgmental opinions. Her approach was to mentally note at the time situations she needed to study; she then wrote the anecdotal observations after school, like the one involving Julian and Noah. Even after the end of the day she found she could remember most of the details! Over a period of two weeks, Juanita kept a journal of the two-part observations, noting her observations and reflections about them for all incidents she thought pertained to her focus.

Results of the Observations

Specifically in terms of her observations of Julian, Juanita observed several episodes where the boy had mistaken unintended behaviors by another child as being done "on purpose" and had become angry. She wondered what prompted these quick, angry responses. She was able to document a pattern, and now she was faced with the challenge of not only solving the immediate situations involving conflict between Julian and other children, but helping Julian deal with his anger. At least, she concluded, she had made progress in terms of understanding this particular child.

In general, Juanita learned from her observations that both boys and girls exhibited mistaken behaviors in the classroom, but that the mistaken behaviors of girls were less noticeable by the teacher. For example, girls engaged in more verbal aggression with their peers whereas boys engaged in more physical aggression. The physical aggression was more difficult for the teacher to redirect or change. [This observation is consistent with research on peer relationships of boys and girls (Grossman & Grossman, 1993; Kindlon & Thompson, 1999; Pollack, 1998).]

Girls in the classroom were more often on-task. The activities and experiences available to them throughout the day held their attention. They would spend long periods of time, typically 15 to 30 minutes, engaged in the same activities, which were often creating in the art area and writing notes, letters, and words in the writing area. Sometimes they would remain for extended periods of time in the dramatic play and housekeeping area of the classroom. Dolls and stuffed animals were popular in both individual and social dramatic play.

Several of the boys on the other hand were less engaged, typically spending fewer than 10 minutes in the usual activities of the class. These guys would go to an activity, look it over, and move on as if they were searching for, but could not find, something to do. When they were "on-task," they spent most of their time in the block area or turning miniature figures and materials into superhero situations and staging make-believe conflicts. When they were not involved with such activities, they tended to engage in rough and tumble play or testing the patience of the teacher and other classmates. [The activity preferences by the girls and boys were consistent with Ligh's research on play choices (Ligh, 2000).]

The observations as well as information gathered from other sources about gender differences focused Juanita's attention on how she could make the classroom more responsive to the needs of the boys and develop strategies for dealing with the mistaken behaviors exhibited by boys in a more positive way.

MAKING THE ENVIRONMENT ENCOURAGING

Through her observations, the workshop she attended, and conversations with her colleagues, Juanita realized that the boys were off-task because they were unable to find interest in many of the classroom activities. A first step Juanita took was to modify the learning environment by considering the needs of specific boys in her classroom. Many boys are not only in need of more physical activity but they may also be developmentally younger

than girls by six to 18 months (Soderman, 1999). The modifications
Juanita made to the classroom supported the activity levels of boys and
their development. The modifications offered more opportunities for:

- indoor and outdoor large motor and whole body experiences.
- sensory exploration and experimentation experiences.
- building and constructing experiences.
- novel dramatic play experiences, games of strategy, and a variety of
  literacy materials.

Juanita focused on these areas of activity because they reflected the
interests of boys. These activities also took place in areas of the classroom
where Juanita tended not to plan. Only through observation did Juanita
begin to see the importance of giving focused attention to these areas.

Indoor and Outdoor Large Motor and Whole Body Experiences

Physical activity is very important to all children, especially young boys.
Most children enjoy using their bodies, running, jumping, and physically
moving their bodies. Juanita's observations guided her to think about
ways to enhance opportunities for large-muscle and whole body experiences in the indoor and outdoor classroom environment. Some of the
strategies that Juanita implemented were to

- *use the outdoor space as a teaching and learning tool.* Juanita planned at
  least one activity in the morning outside. The outdoor activity was
  as simple as taking a nature walk or as complex as creating a water
  system using pipes and joints. She was careful to have the outdoor
  activities happen in small groups, each with an adult. Sometimes
  the small groups went outside separately, other times altogether.

- *plan activities during outdoor play.* Most of the time outdoor play was
  free time with children running, jumping, playing with balls, riding
  tricycles, and swinging. Juanita decided that she would add one
  teacher-planned activity each day. Sometimes the activity was an
  obstacle course or a chasing bubbles or a climbing game. The children could choose whether to join and Juanita was pleased that often many of the boys did. Juanita began seeing outdoor play as an
  extension of her classroom.

- *create a large motor environment indoors.* Juanita decided to work with
  other staff and her director to transform a large storage area into an
  inside large muscle activity room. Large mats, balls, and climbing
  equipment were placed in the room. Juanita used the room for
  tumbling, obstacle courses, dancing and movement, and climbing
  activities.

- *create a large motor center in the classroom.* Juanita added a center in the classroom for large muscle activity. She included beanbags for throwing, carpet squares for jumping, boards for walking, and music for dancing. She alternated this equipment with a (very popular) "physical fitness center" that included a makeshift weight table with "weights" (plastic bottles filled with sand and attached to a sawed-off broom handle), a mini-tramp that the children could use with wrist weights (around their ankles), and a mini-exercise bike one of the parents devised.

- *integrate whole body movements into activities.* Juanita planned activities to include large body movements. In art, children would use feather dusters or actual paintbrushes to paint on large pieces of Plexiglas® or cardboard and with water on the walls outside. Large hollow blocks or cardboard blocks were sometimes used in the block area. Daily music activities almost always involved movement.

Sensory Exploration and Experimentation

Boys enjoy engaging in exploratory and behavior such as digging in sandboxes and taking blocks apart (Grossman & Grossman, 1993). Like many early childhood classrooms, Juanita's classroom had few opportunities for spontaneous and continuous scientific exploration. She made the following changes to her program:

- *explore and experiment.* Juanita decided to create daily opportunities for exploration and experimentation. Each day she planned an activity that allowed children to answer the question, "What happens if . . .?".

- *sensory materials.* Sand and water as well as play dough, clay, glurch (white liquid glue and liquid starch), and commercial liquid starch with white glue ("silly putty") grew to be an integral part of Juanita's classroom. Combining and mixing substances as well as pouring and filling with solids and liquids became a daily occurrence. A parent who was a secondary teacher said he was pleased to see the classroom's "applied chemistry" program.

- *cooking.* Cooking is another way to create opportunities for experimentation and exploration (applied chemistry, physics, math, and biology). Juanita decided that she would plan and implement a simple cooking activity weekly. Preparing fruit salads, vegetable salads, puddings, and pancakes are just a few of the recipes she implemented. In addition, she provided opportunities for children to assist in the making of silly putty, play dough, and goop (powdered starch mixed with water; it has interesting solid/liquid properties).

Building and Construction

Juanita knew that building and construction was a favorite activity of the boys. They spent a significant amount of time playing with blocks, colorful plastic bricks, and other construction materials. Previously, Juanita had not done much planning for these activities. For example, she made blocks available every day but only got involved when she needed to remind the children how to use blocks appropriately. A woodworking area was virtually nonexistent in her classroom. Juanita's art activities were two-dimensional on paper and the boys did not usually actively participate. Juanita decided that she needed to enhance the choices available to children by introducing three-dimensional construction and carpentry activities. She used a variety of strategies to modify the environment to include activities of building and construction. She included pads and pencils so the children could make plans and notes on their building.

- *block building.* Juanita enlarged the space in the classroom for block building. She decided that blocks would be integrated into the classroom. She worked with the children who were interested in building by encouraging free play of the blocks as well as thought-out planning of what they intended to build. Sometimes children drew the plans. Other times the plans were verbal. Juanita also documented children's play in the block area with digital photographs and video. Juanita included both unit blocks and large hollow blocks throughout the year, but regularly changed "accessory items" to fit themes and sustain interest.

- *woodworking.* Juanita introduced woodworking into the classroom. In addition to just having materials available for children to experiment and practice with (enjoyed by both boys and girls), Juanita worked with the children to create developmentally appropriate woodworking projects. She invited parents and local carpenters into the classroom to help with the center. She found that several of the fathers and significant guys were interested in helping to provide materials for this activity area.

- *art and writing.* Juanita added the construction and building materials to the art area thus allowing more choices for whole hand manipulation of materials as well as fine motor manipulation. She added large writing and drawing utensils so the children could choose between wide and narrow. She provided blank sheets of paper stapled down the left side, and introduced them to the children as Action Picture Books that boys and girls could make.

- *tabletop manipulatives were added.* Juanita brought in large manipulatives such as Duplos® in addition to Legos®. She realized that even though boys liked to build, they often did not seem to build easily with Legos®. She made Duplos® as well as Legos® available, concluding that Duplos® would be better for creative work and Legos® would be useful to develop fine motor skills.

There were other changes that Juanita made to the environment that were less dramatic. She decided to change the housekeeping area from time to time, introducing different play themes such as camping, gardening, fishing, medical services, and restaurant. Juanita introduced active but educational computer activities and games of strategy requiring the boys (and girls) to work in cooperative groups.

She reduced time spent in full class and circle times, having the class do stories and focused activities in smaller groups instead. At group story times, informational books on themes of interest to boys were shared in addition to their favorite picture books. Juanita introduced a writing center, and the older boys began making "books" of their "adventures" as spy kids and "Hogwarters."

Juanita found that in the process of making her environment more encouraging for boys, she also empowered the girls in her class to become more active, independent, and creative. The teacher was pleasantly surprised when two parents who were "fitness buffs" complimented Juanita on the physical activity she was encouraging in all of the children. Changing and modifying the program became an ongoing project for Juanita—and as she observed the children in her classroom, she continued to make changes. Most of all, in making these many changes to her program, Juanita modified the actual culture of the classroom. Previously bored and uninvolved, the boys became more engaged, significantly reducing program-influenced mistaken behavior.

Juanita also noticed that the girls, less bothered by frequent conflicts, seemed more relaxed and comfortable in the classroom. Several girls were becoming more engaged in activity areas they hadn't been involved in before such as large-muscle activities and woodworking. Increased physical activity became integrated throughout the curriculum and became more an intentional part of her educational program. She began to think that making these changes was contributing to a more developmentally appropriate program for all the children in the class.

CHANGING INTERVENTION STRATEGIES

The goal of improving the match between young boys and the program is to reduce classroom conflicts, not to think of eliminating all conflicts. While reducing the kinds of conflicts introduced by the educational program, the teacher works to make the conflicts children "naturally" experience into learning opportunities. She makes these teachable moments useful by guiding children in the use of democratic life skills. These skills, the abilities to:

- express strong emotions in nonhurting ways
- appreciate one's own views but also the views of others
- make decisions intelligently and ethically

need to be the educational goals for both girls and boys in a democratic society (Gartrell, 2003).

In order to learn these skills, it is necessary for children to have an opportunity to experience conflict in an environment where adults can help them work on developing appropriate responses to difficult situations. When children are taught appropriate strategies to manage conflict, they are progressing in learning democratic life skills. In the same way that frequent conflict in classrooms creates concern, a classroom where no conflict is observed should also create concern as too controlled and antiseptic.

The next part of the chapter deals with how to interact with boys when they do experience mistaken behavior. Important to keep in mind is that the quality of the interaction between the boy and the teacher is more important than the mistaken behavior in which the boy is involved. (The teacher above all maintains a trust relationship with the child.) The interaction very likely determines how the child will respond in the situation, and feel about himself coming out of the situation. We return to our composite case study of Juanita and her class of 14 three-, four-, and five-year-olds, including 10 boys.

Having begun the changes to her educational program, Juanita became more aware of how the boys were responding when she intervened. Quite different than the girls, some boys would protest loudly or look down so she could not make eye contact with them. Occasional comments from some of the boys were "I'm not listening to you" or "You can't make me." On rare occasions a boy might even strike out and try to hit Juanita.

One day when Juanita was redirecting Jasper, an active four-year-old boy, as a result of a problem in the block building area, he started screaming, calling her an idiot and butthead. Three of his friends who were also upset, began handling the blocks aggressively. When Juanita tried to talk to the boys, they covered their ears with their hands. Juanita finally took Jasper by the hand, moved their conversation to the hallway, and had the assistant teacher talk with the other three boys. At the end of the incident, Juanita wanted to retaliate and punish them for their actions. She felt angry and humiliated by the oppositional and defiant behavior exhibited by the boys. After all, she is the teacher and why would these boys think that they could ignore her and not follow her directions? Juanita decided that she needed to think about what had happened with this group of boys and what she needed to do to make sure that it would not happen again.

After talking with a colleague, Juanita decided to analyze the particular needs of these boys and reflect about the social and emotional development of boys in general. As a result of her reflection, study, and additional discussions with colleagues, Juanita realized that she needed to do more than just change the overall educational program. Juanita's research indicated that boys are more likely to receive harsher discipline than girls (Kindlon & Thompson, 1999). Boys may feel as if they have been singled out or that the teacher's response to the event was unfair. Boys, even young boys, seem to have a strong sense of justice and fair play. Juanita recognized she needed to work on the quality of her interpersonal relations especially during conflicts, as the interpersonal atmosphere influences how children construct feelings about themselves and these feelings impact their behavior (DeVries & Zan, 1994).

Working with her colleagues, Juanita decided upon several strategies to manage mistaken behavior in ways both supportive of the individual and protective of the classroom community. Juanita discovered that these strategies work well with girls as well as boys; however they are essential for helping boys to learn the democratic life skills necessary for social competence. When boys show mistaken behaviors teachers:

- *defuse the situation.* If emotions haven't hit the boiling point, the teacher works to downplay the conflict. Sometimes the situation is accidental, or at least not totally intentional. The teacher points this out and informally mediates: "Carlos, Ephram didn't mean to knock over your tower. He feels bad about it. I wonder how the two of you can fix it?" The teacher identifies and accepts emotions, so the child knows the teacher cares. Example: "Julian, it is all right to cry. That hurt when you fell over Noah's leg. You have a real owie on your knee. Let's get a bandage for that and see how Noah is doing."

- *use humor (but carefully).* Humor is a great tension reliever in conflicts—and is not used enough. Humor suggests that the adult is in charge enough not to get "uptight" and so tells boys they don't have to get "worked up" either. Example: teacher gets down to where two boys are quarreling and says with a smile, "You guys are like gorillas with stomachaches over here. Time to take your Pepto Bismo and get your friendly faces back."

  Humor used with children should be consistent with what we know about each child and their understanding of humor, and should not go beyond their understanding or sound sarcastic. Humor takes thinking on your feet, and for many of us, actual practice. The joke doesn't have to be hilarious—just bring smiles—but it does have to be friendly, not laughing "at" but laughing "with."

- *calm everyone down.* The point of intervention during a conflict is to resolve it with all parties feeling all right about themselves and the resolution. Neither adults nor children can resolve conflicts when emotions are high. A first step, then, is for the teacher to get calm, then help the child or children to calm down. If the child is a boy, the teacher needs to remember that his level of calm may be different from her definition of calm. It is important to let the boy determine when he is calm. In this situation the boy may act or look nonresponsive. The boy may need time to process the intervention by the teacher. He may need time to "check in" with his feelings and regulate his response to the situation. The process may only take a few seconds but sometimes in the fast pace of the early childhood classroom boys are not given the few extra seconds they need.

The teacher supports the boy by identifying and acknowledging feelings, which helps the child feel accepted and regain composure (even when the *behavior* is not accepted). Taking deep breaths is another calming technique. According to Pollack (2001), sometimes a boy may need a timed silence because his timing for expressing hurt feelings may not be consistent with the teacher's timing. A timed silence (alternate term, a "cooling-down time") provides the boy time so that he can deal with the upsetting event alone until he is ready to talk about the event.

Separation should not be an automatic teacher response. When used carefully, separation to calm down for mediation is the one time that leaving a situation is not a punishment (Gartrell, 2003). The adult stays close to the child to help the child regain composure if needed.

- *diagnose the conflict as best you can.* Honestly determine if you know what happened or if you need further information. (Sometimes even children with reputations do things by accident.) Decide what level of firmness you need to use—and how to show warmth with firmness. It is important to remember that boys do not respond well to coercion; therefore it is important that the adult is authoritative rather than authoritarian in his or her response to the conflict (Kindlon & Thompson, 1999; Newberger, 1999; Pollack, 1998). The teacher will need to decide: Is this a situation that calls, for conflict management, a guidance talk, or maybe the quick command of a choice with follow-up? Teachers often must make these decisions very quickly. Remember that the professional teacher learns while teaching, both in the moment and through later reflection.

- *talk in a private manner.* The teacher may want to remove the boy to a private space in the classroom or whisper in his ear how she would like him to change his behavior. There are two reasons for interacting with boys privately. The first is to protect the child from critical self-feelings as a result of being shamed (Pollack, 1998). The second is because boys are likely to respond negatively to adults when they are criticized in front of their peers (Kindlon & Thompson, 1999). Embarrassment "to make a point" usually makes a negative point, one that may stay with a child for years (Gartrell, 2003).

■ *stay away from threats.* Threats set up power struggles that negatively affect both the teacher-child relationship and the likelihood of successful (win–win) resolution of the conflict situation. Instead, if the situation warrants, command choices that the child must make. In commanding choices, the adult poses the more desirable alternative as positively as possible, but accepts the "out choice" if the boy makes it (Gartrell, 2003). To illustrate, the adult does not say, "Martin, either you share the play dough, as I have requested, or I will move you to another area." Rather, the adult puts to the child this choice, "Martin, you choose, you need to share the play dough, or you need to find another activity. You choose. Which will it be?"

Remember that if the boy is upset about the choice or if the boy thinks that the choice is unfair, he may choose not to share the play dough and leave the area. The teacher needs to be ready to accept the decision that the boy makes, and follow up later with a guidance talk. Of course, if the boy keeps the play dough and does not leave, the adult follows through.

■ *follow through.* It is important for teachers to follow through when responding to a boy's mistaken behavior. Boys seem to be sensitive to whether or not adults do what they say they will do. When adults do not follow through, they may lose the boy's respect. Boys may feel as if they do not have to listen because the adult appears powerless to implement their statements. In following through, the teacher models teaching and learning from the conflict. In other words, don't shout across the room for Mitchell to behave and then go on to something else. Walk over, establish your presence, diagnose, interact, and persist. Correct by direction. Stay with it. Lead the boy through the process of learning from the mistake.

■ *use conflict mediation.* When conflicts occur, including with boys, teachers frequently react with punishments like time-out. As other chapters explain, punishments do not teach children the skills they need to solve future conflicts. An important guidance alternative that teachers can employ is *conflict mediation.* Conflict mediation refers to a teacher's intervening in a conflict in order to lead a focused discussion to resolve the problem. Mediation technically is the use of a third party to resolve a conflict between two individuals. Mediation is typically used when a small number of children experience a conflict.

The reason for using conflict mediation is because when children are helped to resolve their disputes, they feel they are fully accepted members of the group. (No one is an outcast for being either a bully or a victim.) They learn democratic life skills, including how to resolve disputes using words, and the classroom becomes a more peaceable place.

As "leaders in charge" the teacher decides whether high-level mediation is needed, in which the teacher is an active coach, or low-level mediation is called for, in which the adult is an "on-hand facilitator." Over time the teacher's goal is to move children to a skill level where they can negotiate a solution to the conflict themselves. Formally or informally, five steps of problem solving are followed:

1. cool down all parties (including yourself)
2. reach agreement about what the problem is
3. brainstorm possible solutions
4. try the most agreeable solution
5. monitor and follow up

Chapter 6 of this book features conflict mediation (using the above "five finger formula"), and it is the guidance intervention of choice with both boys and girls when a small number of children are involved.

■ *hold guidance talks.* A difference between *guidance talks* and conflict mediation is that guidance talks usually are used by a teacher with a single child, either in place of or after mediation. Guidance talks informally follow the five steps of conflict mediation, mentioned above. (They are different than "the lecture.") After emotions have cooled, the teacher:

■ finds out the boy's perception of the reason for the mistaken behavior and his reason for responding as he did.

■ establishes mutual understanding of what happened and how the parties felt.

■ redefines guidelines for acceptable behavior.

■ teaches what the child can do differently next time.

When you think you and the boy have worked the matter through, ask him how he can help the other child feel better (different than forcing an apology). Thank the child for helping to solve the problem, and point out his growing ability to do so. See Chapter 6 for a further discussion of guidance talks.

■ *talk with boys about their emotions.* It is important for adults to talk with boys about their emotions (Kindlon & Thompson, 1999; Polce-Lynch, 2002; Pollack, 1998). Find out how the boy was feeling when you interacted about the mistaken behavior. Sometimes when boys appear to be angry, they really have feelings of pain or fear. They may show anger instead because they perceive that the expression of anger is more socially acceptable. It is important for boys to develop a large repertoire of labels for the emotions they are feeling (Newberger, 1999). Clearly, teaching and learning about emotions and their expression goes beyond conflict interventions by teachers. The curriculum needs to have emotional intelligence—as a component of learning democratic life skills—as an ever-present educational priority beginning with, "It is all right to cry." Many resources are available for teaching and learning about feelings and should be used by teacher-professionals for girls as well as boys.

■ *teach boys to manage their impulses.* Many boys are impulsive; therefore, sometimes when faced with a difficult situation or a conflict, a boy might react by acting out. A helpful approach is to create a strategy with the child, so he knows what he can do instead of hurting others. With warm coaching, one child might say loudly, "I am angry!" (The teacher is then over there quickly.) Another child might leave the conflict and report his feelings to the teacher or go to a "peace island" (an area of the room set up for when a child—or adult—needs a break. Adults are always watching for island visitors who can use a guidance talk). Self-removal is not a cure-all, but can help in teaching individual children to manage those strong feelings by balancing emotions and thought.

■ *manage your own strong emotions.* Even early childhood teachers become angry—and this is often a source of guilt as our image is that we are "ever-nurturing." We do not have to love every child or like it when we see hurting behavior. But we do need to focus our emotions on helping all children, both those who have hurt and been hurt, to learn the skills of getting along. Teachers should model appropriate ways to deal with anger. It is important that children see that adults can become angry, but it is also important that children see adults modeling anger-management behaviors.

■ *nurture boys.* Boys want and need emotional connection (Kindlon & Thompson, 1999; Newberger, 1999; Pollack, 1998). Boys need to be cuddled, held, and responded to with kind words. They need unconditional positive regard from their teachers. When they fall or when a friend uses unkind words or actions, boys need the teacher to respond in a warm, caring, and nurturing manner. Even when a boy is defiant or has hurt another child, we need to let that child know he is still a fully accepted and valued member of our class. He just needs to work on a few things, and it is our job to help. All children, boys as well as girls, need nurturing. They need positive relationships with their teachers.

Change can be a scary and challenging process for teachers. Yet, teachers who make it a priority can change the nature of their teaching and their interpersonal relations with boys. Juanita's story illustrates how teachers can look at themselves and their educational program, and work with fellow staff and colleagues, in order to improve the educational program for young boys. These teachers find that by modifying their educational programs and intervention strategies, they can improve levels of mutual trust, cooperation, and engagement. Moreover, in classrooms where teachers make these changes, girls as well as boys respond to the active programming and positive leadership. With encouragement and education, parents, as well, stand to increase their appreciation of the program and involvement in their children's education, and especially in the education of their boys.

MEN TEACHERS AND THE GUIDANCE OF BOYS

Juanita might well have lamented that "having a man around the room" would give her boys the modeling needed to learn alternatives to their mistaken behavior. In fact, recently one of the authors visited a kindergarten classroom in which both the teacher and student teacher were men. The classroom was comfortable, the activity level busy but on-task, and there seemed to be a sense of pride in both the girls and boys in the room that "these were their guys." For men comfortable with the nurturing and guidance required of the early childhood teacher—and the fortitude to buck the stereotypes—the rewards in the children's responses can be great.

But, being a man in a classroom is clearly not enough. Unless men teachers, as well as women, implement developmentally responsive programs and use guidance in their interpersonal communications, they too will experience problems with the behavior of boys (and girls). In November of 2002, Men in Child Care and Elementary Education Project published an article in *Young Children* that gave helpful and informed treatment to the matter of men in early childhood education. The issue provided a first look at an important study, conducted by Bryan Nelson, entitled *The Importance of Men Teachers and Why There Are So Few* (2002). Three findings from that study are particularly startling.

- Only 4,000 of the total 103,525 membership of NAEYC are men, and only half of this number teach in early childhood classrooms.

- Of the men approximately 360 members are men of color.

- Only 4.95 percent of prekindergarten teachers and 16.2 percent of elementary school teachers are men.

Until society changes so that men feel comfortable in the field (and both men and women are adequately paid), women teachers will be mainly on their own in responding to the needs of young boys, and girls. The approach to teaching boys given in this chapter should help—and should benefit early childhood teachers whatever the gender. Still, picture an education system in which virtually all of the teachers of girls, young and old, happened to be men. Some of these teachers might be attuned to the particular developmental and cultural needs of girls at school, but many, due to experience and their own educations, would not be. Think about it.

In contrast both to the hypothetical situation and the real one, from the summary of Nelson's study, we end this chapter with a soon to be famous quote:

> Imagine walking into an education program in the future and every room you enter there are equal numbers of men and women, teaching, reading or playing with the children. And those teachers, educated and well-paid, are as diverse in characteristics as the children we see in each classroom. With time, resources and persistence, the story can come true. (Nelson, 2002, p. 39)

The reciprocity between men and women in such classrooms would allow teachers of each gender to learn from, and augment the strengths of, the other. Teachers as well as children would stand to grow, learn, and flourish—in ways possible now only in a tiny percentage of classrooms. When teaching teams are comprised of both men and women, teachers may well have to work less arduously to bring about the gains in empathy, self-esteem, and social responsiveness that all early childhood teachers would like to see. But even now, with dedication and effort, teachers of either gender can experience success in using guidance with boys.

End note: *This chapter was excerpted in part in the July, 2003, issue of* Young Children *under the title* Building an Encouraging Classroom with Boys in Mind. *The chapter appears in entirety for the first time in this book.*

REFERENCES

DeVries, R., & Zan, B. (1994). *Moral classrooms, moral children: Creating a constructivist atmosphere in early education.* New York: Teachers College Press.

Gartrell, D. J. (2003). *A guidance approach for the encouraging classroom* (3rd ed.). Clifton Park, NY: Delmar Learning.

Grossman, H., & Grossman, S. (1993). *Gender issues in education.* Boston: Allyn and Bacon.

Kindlon, D., & Thompson, M. (1999). *Raising Cain: Protecting the emotional lives of boys.* New York: Ballantine Books.

Ligh, G. T. (2000). *Traditional gender role behaviors in kindergartners' choices of play activities*. ERIC Document Reproduction Service (FICHE) No. Ed 448918. Publication type DOC: 143 (May, 2000).

Nelson, B. G. (2002). *The importance of men teachers and why there are so few*. Minneapolis, MN: Men in Child Care and Elementary Education Project. http://www.MenTeach.org.

Newberger, E. H. (1999). *The men they will become: The nature and nurture of male character*. Cambridge, MA: Perseus Publishing.

Pastor, P. N., & Reuben, C. A. (2002). Attention deficit disorder and learning disability: United States (1997–98). National Center for Health Statistics, *Vital Health Statistics, 10* (206).

Polce-Lynch, M. (2002). *Boy talk: How you can help your son express his emotions*. Oakland, CA: New Harbinger Publications.

Pollack, W. (1998). *Real boys: Rescuing our sons from the myths of boyhood*. New York: Henry Holt and Company.

Pollack, W. (2001). *Real boys workbook: The definitive guide to understanding and interacting with boys of all ages*. New York: Villard Books.

Soderman, Anne K., et al. (1999). Gender differences that affect emerging literacy in first grade children: The U.S., India, and Taiwan. *International Journal of Early Childhood, 31*(2), 9–16.

CHAPTER 9

Societal Violence and Guidance: Liberation Teaching

QUICK TAKE

Virtually all children in our society experience violence, most indirectly through television, movies, music, and media games, and some directly by being the victims of witnessed or experienced aggression. Children show the effects of violence in our classrooms. At Level One mistaken behavior, they may be overcompetitive in games, or play aggressively with blocks turned into guns and miniature figures into action figures. At Level Two, children may "gang up" against others, or assume the role of action heroes and play too aggressively. At Level Three, they may act out against an unjust world by chronic bullying, temper outbursts, secret hostile acts, self-disparaging behaviors, or frequent fear reactions.

Teachers combat the effects of societal violence by being active leaders for peace in the classroom. Their responses range across the guidance spectrum: creating encouraging classrooms where no child is victimized by violence;

teaching democratic life skills; using liberation teaching with children who have been victimized; and building partnerships with families to do what they can to address violence outside of the classroom.

Chapter 9 looks at societal violence and its effects on children in the classroom, discusses reasons for why children show serious mistaken behavior, acquaints readers with the concept of liberation teaching, and presents a guidance approach to bullying, the in-vogue segue between the effects of societal violence and the classroom. Chapter 9 takes a position that for society to progress, education must change in order to model and teach the practices of peaceable communities.

VIOLENCE AND THE CLASSROOM: A SOCIAL PERSPECTIVE

Compared to the European democracies, Canada, and Japan, ours is an exceedingly violent society (Children's Defense Fund, 2002). Either through direct victimization or indirect media exposure, few children escape societal violence. Writers who believe that our education system must respond to violence generally agree on these facts (Carlsson-Paige & Levin, 1992; Girard & Koch, 1996; Kreidler, 1984; Levin, 1994; and Slaby, Roedell, Arezzo, & Hendrix, 1995):

- Social conflicts—disagreements, disputes—happen all the time; they are part of life for children and adults.

- Popular culture glorifies violence in ways that make civil problem solving difficult to teach and learn.

- Virtually all children are touched by violence, even if it is "background violence" through exposure to television and video games, the content of which is often unmonitored or is controlled by adult interests.

- Some children, touched deeply by violence, are affected for their whole lives—unless they experience comprehensive intervention while they are young.

- If we as a society are to increase our capacity to resolve conflicts peacefully, we need to provide comprehensive educational programs for our children, beginning while they are young, in the home and in school.

In this discussion, we take a broad definition of violence, to include acts of rejection and aggression that result in: arousal of stress with attendant emotions of anxiety, anger, fear, and confusion; debasement of the child's self-concept; and some degree of impairment in healthy brain development. At bottom, the act of violence is the assertion of will by a more powerful individual against a less powerful individual, without regard for physical and psychological well-being.

These several writers basically agree that for society to become more peaceful, a change is necessary in how we look at education. Teaching for emotional development—stressing resiliency, interpersonal and intrapersonal intelligence, democratic life skills—whatever terms one is comfortable with—must become at least as important as scores on standardized tests. Yet, this change in our schools will only occur as families demand it, and much parent education about violence has yet to happen.

Effects of Violence in the Classroom

Behavior for any individual is the complex product of development, personality (including disposition), past experiences, and perceptions of present circumstances. Researchers have identified patterns of classroom behavior that are more likely to occur when violence is present in a child's life (Gootman, 1993; Lowenthal, 1999). In fact, adults see the effects of violence in children's behavior every day in early childhood classrooms. Violence in its many forms is the major cause of serious mistaken behavior. The effects especially of direct violence, witnessed or directly experienced, are striking. In a recent review of the literature, Lowenthal (1999) provides a graphic summary adapted here:

- difficulty in managing emotions. Past experiences may overwhelm the child's ability to handle emotions, especially those associated with past traumatic events. For these children, gaining a measure of self-regulation—learning to manage anger—is an important first step in learning life skills. At times, one-on-one assistance becomes necessary. Such efforts as visiting "worry teachers" and classroom "comfort corners" can address these situations (Gartrell, 2003).

- avoidance of intimacy. Loss of trust causes children to view intimate relationships as increasing their vulnerability and lack of control. "To avoid intimacy, children may withdraw, avoid eye contact, be hyperactive, or exhibit inappropriate behaviors" (Lowenthal, 1999). A motivation for mistaken behaviors, then, may be to avoid forming close relationships, which in the past the child has found profoundly painful.

- provocative behaviors. Violent reactions may be the main form of adult attention the child has known. For these kids, provoking negative reactions becomes a learned behavior. It is how they have learned to relate to adults.

    From another perspective, a psychological reaction to violence is chemical brain activity that numbs the individual to the extreme emotions violent experiences arouse. Over time this defensive reaction by the brain wears off, and the emotional pain returns. Lowenthal (1999) suggests that without therapy, children feel a human need to again numb themselves. By acting "provocatively and aggressively," children seek to produce the extreme reactions that cause renewal of the "self-anesthetizing" process. (Later drug use may serve the same purpose.) In early childhood classrooms, these understandings bring new meaning to the need for teachers to "keep your cool."

■ disturbances in the attachment process. The attachment process is the long-term bond that forms between a child and primary caregivers. Abuse and neglect make attachment difficult, due to children's feelings of mistrust, unworthiness, anger, and anxiety. These feelings may cause children to become hostile toward adults who genuinely wish to build positive attachments. Building positive attachments under such circumstances becomes a challenging but essential task.

■ effects on cognition and learning. Over time violent experiences cause children's emotion-based brain reactions to overwhelm cognitive processes. Mental functions involved in learning become more difficult (LeDoux, 1996). At the same time, self-perceptions tell the child that she is incapable of learning and unworthy of teacher assistance, lowering motivation levels. "On average, abused, maltreated, or neglected children score lower on cognitive measures and demonstrate poorer school achievement compared to their non-abused peers of similar socioeconomic backgrounds." (Lowenthal, 1999, p. 206)

This list of children's reactions to violence is daunting indeed. Gootman (1993) agrees with Lowenthal (1999) that teachers must step forward and be *enlightened witnesses* for children who have experienced violence. Teachers who are enlightened witnesses affirm the goodness within each child and that the child is not to blame for the violence experienced (Gootman, 1993). Such teachers work to build positive attachments and make the classroom a trustworthy place where learning can happen. Against the odds, by encouraging *resiliency*—personal strength that promotes self-healing—they practice *liberation teaching.*

Assessing the Effects of Violence, by the Levels

Using the three levels of mistaken behavior as guideposts (introduced in Chapter 2), the following classroom behaviors are typical of children who have been affected by violent experiences. Mistaken behaviors at Levels One and Two are more common in children who are influenced by indirect "background violence." Level Three mistaken behaviors are typical of children directly victimized by violence in the home or community. Included are brief considerations for interpreting these mistaken behaviors.

Level One: Experimentation Mistaken Behavior

The following behaviors are Level One: if they are shown once in a while by a child, but not on a repeated, emotionally "driven" basis: A child makes play guns and weapons out of "nonviolent" materials such as blocks, Lincoln logs, and other materials. A child draws pictures with violent themes. A child initiates *rough-and-tumble play*—perhaps linked to superheroes—such as wrestling, chase, and "guns" (Boyd, 1997). A child "plays rough" with puppets, dolls, and miniature figures. A child is surprisingly competitive in play situations. (These behaviors become mistaken, of course, only when they threaten harm or disruption in the class.)

Considerations: Boyd comments that "Part of the human condition is to fear and to desire mastery of that fear" (1997). In the relatively powerless position of childhood, children imagine themselves less vulnerable and more powerful through play that involves make-believe. Children often use art and individual dramatic play with figures for this purpose.

Rough-and-tumble play also helps accomplish this goal. At the same time, roughhousing actually may assist children to build friendships, establish dominance patterns (which can actually reduce conflict by defining power structures within a group), and facilitate social skills—such as interpreting own and others emotions (Boyd, 1997). A child who makes a situation competitive and "wins" asserts personal power. Children at Level One are showing reactions to violence experiences that may be worrisome to them. Regular repetition of these behaviors indicates different motivation, however, and the behaviors are the result either of the immediate influence of others or deep unmet needs.

Level Two: Socially Influenced Mistaken Behavior

One way that children show societal violence in their behavior is when they are *influenced by others* to join in rough-and-tumble play and "mischief." This social influence is often twofold, within the classroom by influential peers who "start" the play, and from outside the class by neighbors and family members who influence the child toward the mistaken behavior. Boyd identifies *superhero play,* in which children identify with action heroes and play more roughly than they would otherwise, as a common variation of rough-and-tumble play (Boyd, 1997). In this case the outside influence is not real people but media creations. Classic older superheroes are Superman and Wonder Woman; influences now fading somewhat are the Morphin Power Rangers and the Ninja Turtles. Recent additions to the panoply are WWE wrestling characters and the rejuvenated characters from movies of Spider Man and the Incredible Hulk.

Mimicking ostracism they have experienced outside of the classroom, some children notoriously show another type of socially influenced mistaken behavior. They stigmatize other children by excluding them from activities, calling them names, and generally oppressing them. Often a group of children shows this behavior toward a child or vulnerable group in an attempt to establish "in-groups" and "out-groups." When an individual child "picks on" another, the behavior is typically called bullying. In an individual situation at the experimentation level, a child may show domineering behavior. Often, as mentioned, there is an obvious social influence at work—the behavior has been learned. When a child stigmatizes another as the result of a need to act out against a hostile world, the child is showing Level Three mistaken behavior. The oppressive behavior then appears to be strongly emotional and is often repeated—ironically making the "bullying" child vulnerable for stigmatization by others (Surgeon General's Report, 1999). When ostracism is a Level Two behavior, children more easily learn socially acceptable alternatives than when deep unmet needs are involved.

Considerations: Teachers need to actively support children who are vulnerable for stigma, because of particular appearances, abilities, or behaviors. Unless the teacher creates a spirit of mutual affirmation in the classroom, some children are likely to assert their power by affiliating with others in oppressive acts. When stigma occurs, direct violence is happening in the classroom, and the teacher must show firm leadership—by class meetings, ethics instruction, guidance talks, and conflict management. In an encouraging classroom the teacher does not allow any child to be stigmatized.

Level Three: Strong-Needs Mistaken Behavior

A major cause of Level Three mistaken behavior is direct violence experienced by a child. The harm may be physical, psychological, or both. When the emotional motivation for a behavior is intense and the mistaken behavior continues over time, any of the types of mistaken behavior mentioned previously can be an indication of strong unmet needs and so be Level Three. Examples are violent pictures drawn repeatedly, rough-and-tumble play that often becomes hurtful, and bullying that is continuing and severe. Other common indicators are children who repeatedly lose emotional balance, unexpectedly try to harm others, influence others to serious acts, withdraw from situations, or show marked anxiety (Gootman, 1993).

Considerations: Our goal with children who are the victims of direct violence is to help them build resiliency. A first step in this process is to establish an attachment with the child in order to help her or him find trust in the classroom environment (Gootman, 1993). Interventions must be firm but friendly to retain the child's sense of trust. A child who has experienced violence may have lost any ability to define and meet limits. When we enforce limits nonpunitively, the child eventually will appreciate the safety that our limits provide. Children who show Level Three behaviors require comprehensive intervention strategies (the subject of the next chapter) that involve teachers, family members, and often other professionals (Gootman, 1993). *Liberation teaching* occurs in the active support, encouragement, and guidance of all children showing vulnerabilities in the classroom, but especially children showing Level Three mistaken behavior.

SERIOUS MISTAKEN BEHAVIOR: A PSYCHOLOGICAL PERSPECTIVE

Coming out of the Middle Ages, a common idea about the nature of children continues to this day. It is that while all children have wayward tendencies, some children, like adults, are on balance "good" and other children, due to their personal constitutions, tend to be "bad" (Greenberg, 1988). In this view of human nature, parents and teachers can change human nature slightly, but not fundamentally. Midway through the 19th century this view was being assailed in the writings of progressive educators such as Froebel, originator of the kindergarten, and into the 20th century in the writings of Montessori, Dewey, and Piaget (Gartrell, 2003).

For his times, Froebel "nailed" the position against a predetermined human nature, writing of the impact of the teacher on the life of the child:

> It is certainly true that as a rule the child is first made bad by some other person, often by the educator himself. This can happen when everything which the child does out of ignorance or thoughtlessness or even from a keen sense of right and wrong is attributed to an intention to do evil. Unhappily there are among teachers those who always see children as mischievous, spiteful . . . whereas others see at most an over-exuberant sense of life or a situation which has got out of hand. (as cited in Lilley, 1967, p. 135)

Froebel was arguing for a human nature that involves a positive, developing potential, greatly affected by interactions with others, in this case teachers. In the common language of this classic debate, his position was "nurture over nature." The debate has swayed back and forth since, of course, towards "nature" in the misapplied theories of "social Darwinism" (Gould, 1996) and toward nurture in the behavioral psychology of the mid-20th century.

In recent years the great beginnings that neuroscientists have made in the study of brain development have added to the discussion. This research has documented that when children have positive attachments with adults and a nurturing learning environment, their brains make countless, vital connections across billions of neurons (brain cells) in an optimum fashion (Diamond & Hopson, 1998). Children's capacity for the healthy development and expression of thoughts and feelings is enhanced.

Supported by brain research, the guidance perspective is that there is no such thing as a bad child, only children with bad problems, too big for children to handle on their own. In the face of life difficulties for which they cannot find relief, children experience stress. Children in chronic stress become oversensitized to a need for defensive reactions. They tend to view minor social problems as major conflicts and react accordingly. They show repeated frustration, aggression, and "oppositional behaviors"—or in the other extreme, introjected feelings of inadequacy and isolation from the group. Over time, if the stress is not alleviated, hormones secreted within the brain affect the way children process thoughts and feelings (LeDoux, 1996), with eventual loss in the ability to respond "intelligently and ethically."

Their small amount of development and experience makes young children who show chronic stress difficult to work with. Their requests for help often take the form of mistaken behaviors. A young child can neither fully conceptualize nor articulate a rational response to hurts experienced—difficult for many adults as well. A teacher probably will not hear a child say, "Being prevented by my friends from joining them in the play-store causes me considerable agitation. Would you be kind enough, dear teacher, to mediate a solution to this problem that all of us will find satisfactory?" (Author grins here.) More likely a child, hurt and angry, swipes boxes and cans off the shelf of the store and hits when another child tries to stop her, or perhaps sits and cries.

A prime cause of stress in children is rejection by significant others, both adults and peers. *(The developmental egocentrism of young children causes them to interpret violence as rejection in the extreme.)* In the classroom children who experience repeated conflicts are often *stigmatized,* or negatively separated from the group (rejected), as a result of their behavior. In other words the expression of hurts caused by rejection outside of the classroom results in further rejection within the classroom. Personality labeling of such children tends to mark them across their school years and endangers their futures (Ladd & Price, 1987).

BULLYING AND THE GUIDANCE RESPONSE

Bullying has become a hot topic in American education, and for good reason. Bullying is societal violence brought into the classroom. Recent studies, including a large study from the National Institutes of Child Health and Human Development (Nansel et al, 2001) indicates that youth who bully have more behavior problems, regard school more negatively, and are at greater risk for legal problems as adults. Children who are bullied "generally show higher levels of insecurity, anxiety, depression, loneliness, unhappiness, physical and mental symptoms, and low self esteem." Witnesses to bullying as well are affected (Nansel et al., 2001). While the national study focused on adolescents rather than young children, Froschl and Sprung (1999) discuss bullying in early childhood education. These authors emphasize the importance of comprehensive prevention and intervention with young children to prevent the onset of the long-term consequences of bullying.

This discussion of bullying has three parts. Part one discusses bullying as the classic example of child-initiated stigma in the educational setting; part two analyzes bullying in relation to the three levels of mistaken behavior; part three emphasizes the importance of a comprehensive approach to prevention and intervention rooted in liberation teaching.

Bullying as Violence that Causes Stigma

The national study on bullying gives an often-quoted definition:

> Bullying is a specific type of aggression in which (1) the behavior is intended to harm or disturb, (2) the behavior occurs repeatedly over time, and (3) there is an imbalance of power, with a more powerful person or group attacking a less powerful one. (Nansel et al, 2001)

While the definition of bullying implies events over time, both Nansel et al., (2001) in the National Study and Froschl and Sprung (1999) indicate that even single occurrences of bullying can have detrimental effects.

Not all children are equally vulnerable for bullying. Behavioral and physical factors make children particularly susceptible to bullying (Nansel et al., 2001). Children are bullied more if they are isolated from others in the classroom or if their own behavior is chronically aggressive. (The National Study expresses particular concern about children who both bully and are the victims of bullying.) Children *stigmatized* (negatively separated from the group) due to unusual physical appearance or due to a disability are also more likely to be bullied. Bullying tends to further stigmatize children already vulnerable for stigma.

Froschl and Sprung (1999) point out that in one study 78% of K–3 children who initiated bullying were boys, though girls and boys equally were likely to be the targets. This finding was similar in the national study, which provided the additional data that bullying by boys was more likely to deteriorate into physical aggression while the bullying of girls was more likely to include taunting, exclusion, and gossip (Nansel et al., 2001).

Bullying as Levels of Mistaken Behavior

Level One is experimentation level mistaken behavior. A child picks on another child, calls another child a name, or excludes another child from play in order to find out what will happen. From the statistics, children who initiate bullying are likely to be boys. Level One bullying may happen "out of the blue," and in fact be a first occurrence for the child. Yet, this is not a time for the teacher to conclude, "It is just once and boys will be boys." According to Froschl and Sprung (1999), a common adult response to bullying is to ignore it. Adults condone bullying when they fail to recognize it or deny the importance of intervention when they do recognize it (Froschl & Sprung, 1999). The child who tries out bullying and is not guided to learn from the experience may conclude that bullying is tolerated. For this child, the teacher may cause bullying to become a Level Two mistaken behavior.

Level Two is socially influenced mistaken behavior. As suggested, bullying becomes Level Two when a child has been reinforced for bullying behavior. This happens most frequently when a teacher ignores, and so condones, experimentation bullying. It also can happen if a teacher overreacts with punishment to the child doing the bullying. The child then learns that bullying is a way of achieving attention, albeit negative, and may repeat its use.

A second way that children show Level Two bullying is if they are influenced by peers to join in the stigmatization of a vulnerable child. Group bullying through name-calling, ostracism, or even aggression is a pernicious, if common, form. By identifying with a group against a child, participating children feel a sense of belonging and power—which they may be denied in teacher-led, organized activities.

Level Three, strong-needs mistaken behavior, is due to trouble in a child's life that is beyond his capacity to cope with and understand. Children at Level Three often show "classic bullying" with the emotional intensity and persistence that are associated with this act. Children who show repeated bullying may become the targets of bullying themselves—the group of high concern in the national study. With more social savvy, some children at Level Three instigate others to join in the bullying, bringing to the clique an emotional intensity that elevates annoyance bullying to the pernicious.

At any of the levels of mistaken behavior, conflict management is the intervention of choice in the event of bullying. Mediation gives the targeted child a chance for needed self-assertion and teaches the child doing the bullying that only friendly behaviors belong in the classroom. If bullying becomes frequent, class meetings as well are called for. Prevention, by activities promoting friendliness and inclusiveness, also is needed. Parents may be enlisted to bring the message of friendliness "home" to children as well. The next section discusses the use of guidance to prevent bullying.

A Three-Pronged Approach to Prevention

Writers about bullying agree that the key to solving problems of bullying in the classroom lies with the teacher. They agree that the teacher's responses must show active leadership and be comprehensive (Beane, 2000; Froschl & Sprung, 1999; Hoover & Oliver, 1996; Nansel et al., 2001).

With the class, the teacher works on *prevention* by talking and teaching about bullying and the need for friendliness. The teacher uses children's books, puppet and role plays, story pictures, experience charts, journals, and class meetings to teach children the importance of empathy and inclusion (Beane 2000; Froschl & Sprung, 1999; Hoover & Oliver, 1996). The teacher and children together make guidelines to define the spirit of encouragement. The teacher excludes competitive practices in instruction and games that set children against each other and put an artificial premium on performance. She designs activities and encourages cooperation and relationships that go across genders, "because anyone can be friends in our classroom, girls and girls, girls and boys, boys and girls, and boys and boys" (Froschl & Sprung, 1999).

The teacher holds class meetings to assess and further the development of a cooperative group spirit. To lessen tension and aid group problem solving, she may use relaxation activities and soothing sound effects, like flowing water (Froschl & Sprung, 1999). The prevailing intent of the meetings is to accept and celebrate human differences in the class. The adult teaches children that if they cannot stop it themselves, it is all right to report bullying. In the encouraging classroom, bullying does not have a "code of silence."

The adult may teach the use of de-escalating words or actions for children to use (Gartrell, 2003). (When a toddler got into a habit of biting to get his way, a teacher taught the other children, if threatened by the child, to hold up their hands and say "Stop"! This defensive action disrupted the impulse of the child who was biting, and alerted the teachers to intervene. They encouraged the child to use words too and reinforced the need for friendliness.) The adult teaches that children have a right not to be bullied, and at the same time a child who is bullying needs to be accepted as a full member of the class. This challenging balance is at the heart of liberation teaching.

With the child, the teacher uses observation and conversation to assess whether the bullying is the result of experimentation, social influence, or deep unmet needs. She also uses her relationship to help a child prone to bullying find a sense of belonging and self-esteem through creative and cooperative activities. She knows that the child needs to learn alternative ways to gain power and prestige. She uses conflict management to teach children involved in a situation that they both have rights, they just need to express them in friendly ways.

For children at Level Three who are bullying, teachers use the crisis intervention techniques and comprehensive intervention strategies discussed in Chapter 10. The teacher intervenes in firm but friendly ways (using conflict management and guidance talks), seeks more information, develops her relationship with the child, helps the child find success in the program, involves fellow staff and parents, and, if necessary, implements a formal plan to reach these goals.

Most of all, the teacher is vigilant, ever aware of the possibility of bullying behavior. In fact, the liberating teacher has a zero tolerance for bullying. But she also has a zero tolerance for disqualifying any child from full participation in the class. When she sees bullying, she acts to make it a teaching opportunity because she knows that all children can learn democratic life skills. Some children will just take longer to learn than others.

A necdote

I walked out onto the playground and immediately saw that an older girl from another room was hitting Kevin. Kevin stood against the fence with his arms up over his head. I hurried over and arrived at the same time as the teacher of the other child. She pulled the child off of Kevin, and we both knelt down, holding each child, to talk to them. Before either of us said anything, Kevin looked at the other child and said, "It made me very mad when you hit me." He told the older girl, "You're supposed to use words, not hit." The girl from the other class did not respond in any way during the discussion. I thanked Kevin for using his words and not hitting back. The teacher stayed to talk with the girl. She later told me that she and her teaching team had scheduled a "staffing" concerning her that day and would meet with the parents soon. (Gartrell, 2000)

With staff, the teacher works for a unified, program-wide approach to bullying. If all teachers in a school or program team together to build encouraging classrooms, develop positive relations with parents, handle mistaken behavior with guidance, and take a planned approach to bullying that includes both systematic prevention and intervention, stigmatizing behaviors will decrease (Beane, 2000; Hoover & Oliver, 1996). Policies addressing bullying/friendliness issues need to be clear to children and adults alike, and enforced in firm but friendly ways (Beane, 2000). Administrators need to be visible regarding their leadership with guidance policies in relation to bullying. Both students and teachers need to participate in the policy/guidelines process. "Cohesiveness among the teaching staff and the principal [or director] relates to less violence" (Beane, 2000, p. 6). Working with fellow staff, the liberating teacher accomplishes what she cannot on her own.

With parents, the teacher starts from the beginning of the year to build positive relations and to communicate that parents and teacher are on the same team. She makes guidance priorities, including teaching democratic life skills, known to parents right away. She shares guidelines with parents that she and the class have developed. She involves parents in simple activities with their children that encourage empathy building and the acceptance of human differences (Froschl & Sprung, 1999).

When problems involving bullying become serious, the teacher involves parents. She holds conferences for face-to-face discussion, using reflective listening, compliment sandwiches, and social problem solving. If differing viewpoints about bullying grow evident, the teacher works to make them creative differences rather than negative dissonance (Gartrell, 2003). She may involve a third party to mediate differences and to take leadership in implementing an individual guidance plan. A personal support system including fellow staff, family, and friends allows the teacher to persist in the risks and challenges in eliminating bullying from the classroom.

Reaching a child who bullies, is bullied, or both—and helping the child to overcome—is the goal and reward of the teacher in the encouraging classroom. Beth Wallace's story of Jeremiah wonderfully illustrates this point.

A necdote

Jeremiah was almost three when I started teaching at the center. He was one of those very physical kids, whose feelings and thoughts always moved through his body first. He'd had a turbulent life and when I came to the center, he was living mostly with his mom, and some with his dad. They were separated and neither made very much money. Jeremiah was a shiningly bright kid, curious about and interested in everything, who loved stories and connected with others with his whole heart. He knew so much about the natural world and was observant and gentle with animals, insects, and plants.

When I first started working with Jeremiah, he had a lot of angry outbursts. The center used time out at that point (the dreaded "green chair") and Jeremiah spent considerable time there. While I was at the center, we moved away from using time outs. Instead we introduced a structured system of problem solving called "peer problem solving" developed by a Montessori teacher in New Hampshire. By the time Jeremiah graduated to kindergarten, we had been using the system for three years, and he was one of the experts.

One day, I overheard a fracas in the block corner. I stood up to see what was going on, ready to intervene. The youngest child in the room, who was just two and only talking a little bit, and one of the four year olds were in a dispute over a truck. There was an obvious imbalance of power, and I took a step forward, ready to go to their aid. Then I saw Jeremiah approach them.

"What's going on?" he asked (my standard opening line). He proceeded to facilitate a discussion between the two children that lasted for five minutes. He made sure both kids got a chance to speak; he interpreted for the little one. "Jordan, what do you think of that idea?" he asked. Jordan shook his head and clutched the truck tighter. "I don't think Jordan's ready to give up the truck yet," he told the four year old.

It was amazing. Jeremiah helped the kids negotiate an agreement, and then he walked away with a cocky tilt to his head I'd never seen before. His competence was without question; his pride was evident. (Gartrell, 2000. Thanks to Beth Wallace for this anecdote.)

LIBERATION TEACHING

The concept of *liberation teaching* has sources as varied as the social psychology of Goffman (1963), the social commentary of Gottlieb (1973) and Boyer (1992), Catholic theology of the 1960s and 1970s, and the family psychology of Faber and Mazlich (1974). A teacher who is liberating actively assists a child vulnerable for stigma to develop the life skills and outlook necessary to become an accepted group member (Gartrell, 2003). She or he creates a spirit of community within the class (an encouraging classroom) that fundamentally aids in this effort.

Liberation teaching shows itself both in the teacher's immediate response to conflicts, especially with children who are vulnerable for rejection, and in the overall guidance strategy the teacher uses with these children. Liberation teaching means seeking to understand what is bothering a child, and helping the child resolve both the immediate conflict and the underlying life problem. Only with progress in these efforts can the child find acceptance in the classroom community. With social acceptance the child is able to avoid the lasting pitfalls of stigma: a cycle of rejection, stress, negative self-labeling, eventual out-group peer identification (with gangs or cults), and violence against one's self and the community. From my book, *What the Kids Said Today,* I would like to illustrate an example of liberation teaching. In this anecdote, Kaylynn responds to a child in conflict with two classmates (Gartrell, 2000, pp. 139–140):

I heard the words, "Shut up," and walked around the corner to the bathroom to find out what was happening.

Shayna was sitting in the corner crying. I said, "Shayna, why are you crying?"

Shayna said, "Amanda and Christine said they aren't my friends anymore."

I asked her if she told them to shut up. Shayna said yes. I told her I was sorry that what they had said made her feel sad and angry, but we don't use those words in our center. (Amanda and Christine had been watching and listening to us talk.) I explained to Shayna that maybe next time she could tell the girls it made her sad to hear they didn't want to be her friends. I told Amanda and Christine that Shayna was feeling sad. They came over to Shayna and gave her a hug and said they were sorry.

A little later, Shayna walked over to the breakfast table. She started crying again. I asked, "Is something making you feel sad, Shayna?"

She said, "I miss my Daddy." Her father was killed in a car accident a few months before.

I sat down on a chair, hugging and holding her. I said, "Shayna, my daddy died when I was a little girl and it made me very sad, too. I am so glad you told me why you were crying." We sat by each other and ate breakfast.

Shayna went to the housekeeping area for choice time. Later in the day she came up to me and said, "I'm over my daddy now."

I said, "Shayna, it's OK to feel sad about missing your daddy. I still miss my dad. If you need a hug or want to talk, you come and tell me."

REFLECTION

This incident gave me the "chills." I felt sad for Shayna, but I also felt good that she was able to verbally express her feelings about her father's death. This experience reinforced the importance of listening to young children. As a teacher I need to take the time to listen and "open the door" for these opportunities to be a listener. Shayna had a need to talk about her father's death. Hopefully Shayna can talk more about her feelings, and she knows that I care about her.

Later I talked with Shayna's Mother about the incident and Shayna's behavior at home. With Shayna's Mother's approval, we asked our mental health counselor to observe and talk with Shayna the next time he came to our center. I also gave Shayna more personal attention and made other staff aware of the incident. The next day Shayna sat on my lap at the play dough table. We made cookies together.

For me, what is liberating in this situation is that Kaylynn intervened in a way that kept Shayna's trust. Despite setting a limit about the un-friendly words and teaching an alternative behavior, Kaylynn conveyed to Shayna that she cared about the child. Her message was clearly accepted, because Shayna came to the teacher later, when she needed comfort.

Note too that Kaylynn focused on helping Shayna cope with her loss—the death of her Dad that Shayna may have experienced as ultimate rejection—rather than on Shayna's mistaken behavior. A guidance prin-ciple is that building a healthy attachment with a child is necessary to help the child learn socially responsive behaviors—something that liberating teachers know and do.

Even with behavior more extreme than that showed by Shayna, the teacher seeks to understand the child in the situation and respond to the child in a way that affirms and teaches. When a teacher reaches a child who otherwise might be rejected by the classroom community and teaches the child to cope, stress levels go down and healthy brain func-tioning is buttressed. Coaching a child toward resiliency, the heart of lib-eration teaching, can turn around a child's life. The significance of early childhood education is that through work with the child and the family, many traumas of childhood can be ameliorated before they have lasting developmental effects. Unattended, the unhealed adult may show the very behaviors that "prove" to others that some children are destined to be "bad guys."

End Note: *This chapter is adapted from Chapter Twelve "Liberation Teaching: A Guidance Response to Violence in Society" in Gartrell, D. J. (2003).* A Guidance Approach for the Encouraging Classroom *(3rd ed.). Clifton Park; NY: Delmar Learning.*

REFERENCES

Beane, A. L. (2000). *Bully free classroom.* Minneapolis, MN: Free Spirit Publishing.

Boyd, B. J. (1997). Teacher response to superhero play: To ban or not to ban. *Childhood Education, 74*(1), 23–28.

Boyer, E. L. (1992). *Ready to learn.* The Carnegie Foundation for the Advancement of Teaching. New York: Carnegie Foundation.

Carlsson-Paige, N., & Levin, D. E. (1992). Making peace in violent times: A constructivist approach to conflict resolution. *Young Children, 48*(1), 4–13.

Children's Defense Fund. (2002). *The state of children in America's union 2002.* Washington, DC: Children's Defense Fund.

Diamond, M., & Hopson, J. (1998). *Magic trees of the mind: How to nurture your child's intelligence, creativity, and healthy emotions from birth through adolescence.* New York: Dutton.

Faber, A., & Mazlich, E. (1974). *Liberated parents, liberated children.* New York: Avon Books.

Froschl, M., & Sprung, B. (1999). On purpose: Addressing teasing and bullying in early childhood. *Young Children, 54*(2), 70–72.

Gartrell, D. J. (2000). *What the kids said today: Using classroom conversations to become a better teacher.* St. Paul, MN: Redleaf Press.

Gartrell, D. J. (2003). *A guidance approach for the encouraging classroom* (3rd ed.). Clifton Park, NY: Delmar Learning.

Girard, K., & Koch, S. J. (1996). *Conflict resolution in the schools.* San Francisco: Jossey-Bass.

Goffman, E. (1963). *Stigma: Notes on the management of spoiled identity.* Englewood Cliffs, NJ: Prentice-Hall.

Gootman, M. E. (1993). Reaching and teaching abused children. *Childhood Education, 70*(1), 15–19.

Gottlieb, D. (Ed.). (1973). *Children's liberation.* Englewood Cliffs, NJ: Prentice-Hall.

Gould, S. J. (1996). *The mis-measure of Man* (Rev. ed.). New York: W. W. Norton.

Greenberg, P. (1988). Avoiding "me against you" discipline. *Young Children, 43*(1), 24–31.

Hoover, J. H., & Oliver, R. (1996). *The bullying prevention handbook.* Bloomington, IN: National Education Service.

Kreidler, W. J. (1984). *Creative conflict resolution: More than 200 activities for keeping peace in the classroom.* Glenview, IL: Scott, Foresman.

Ladd, G. W., & Price, J. M. (1987). Predicting children's social and emotional adjustment following the transition from preschool to kindergarten. *Child Development, 58,* 986–992.

LeDoux, J. (1996). *The emotional brain.* New York: Simon & Schuster.

Levin, D. (1994). *Teaching young children in violent times: Building a peaceable classroom.* Cambridge, MA: Educators for Social Responsibility.

Lilley, I. M. (Ed.). (1967). *Friedrich Froebel: A selection of his writings.* London: Cambridge University Press.

Lowenthal, B. (1999). Effects of maltreatment and ways to promote children's resiliency. *Childhood Education, 74*(4), 204–209.

Nansel, T. R., Overpeck, M., Pilla, R. S., Ruan, W. J., Simons-Morton, B., & Scheidt, P. (2001). Bullying behaviors among U.S. youth: Prevalence and association with psychosocial adjustment. *Journal of the American Medical Association, 285*(16), 2094–2100.

Slaby, R. G., Roedell, W. C., Arezzo, D., & Hendrix, K. (1995). *Early violence prevention.* Washington, DC: National Association for the Education of Young Children.

Surgeon General. (1999). *Surgeon general's report on violence.* Washington, DC: Department of Health and Human Services.

CHAPTER 10

Strong-Needs Mistaken Behavior: Strategies for Crisis Management and Comprehensive Guidance

QUICK TAKE

Besides Chapter 8, "Guidance with Boys," this is the chapter you may have been waiting for: a discussion of what to do when children experience serious conflicts in your classroom. Because you are professionals and not technicians, you already know not to expect magic answers. Instead, Chapter 10 offers strategies for your consideration about how to intervene firmly when things get tough, but in ways that teach rather than punish. Guidance is, after all, just good teaching—from a mind to a mind, but also from a heart to a heart (and sometimes, as this chapter explores, from a will to a will).

The chapter begins with a guidance perspective on classroom conflicts; follows with a recommendation of four different crisis management techniques; and concludes with a case study in comprehensive guidance. No magic answers are to be found, but my hope is that you will discover helpful information, for your everyday use when situations get tough, and for your continuing development as a guidance professional.

In an encouraging classroom teachers move away from judging children on the basis of reputations about their behaviors, expecting misbehavior from some children and "nice" behavior from others. They accept all children as full and contributing members of the classroom community (Greenberg, 1988). They look at the problems children show as mistaken behaviors made in the course of learning democratic life skills: conflicts to be managed, resolved, and learned from. (See Chapter 5 for a discussion of democratic life skills—the outcomes we work toward when using guidance.)

In the encouraging classroom teachers work hard to prevent conflicts that their daily teaching practices may actually cause, through

- unrealistic behavioral expectations
- negative judgments about children's characters
- stereotyped cultural expectations
- overreliance on large groups
- inappropriate academic expectations
- unreliable program structure and daily scheduling

At the same time teachers recognize that even in the most developmentally appropriate classrooms some conflict—the result of everyday disagreements as well as strong unmet needs—is inevitable. Teaching young children democratic life skills through the management of such conflicts is seen as an essential part of, and not a deviation from, the basic educational program.

This is not to say that teachers take conflicts for granted. While professional teachers accept that conflicts happen in all early childhood classrooms, they do not accept that conflicts have value in themselves, or that conflicts should necessarily run a "natural course."

A conflict is a situation in which the parties experience a disagreement and cannot easily resolve it. During conflicts all involved are at-risk for psychological and sometimes physical harm. This is clearly the case for children in conflicts with more powerful peers. But children who initiate conflicts in order to assert their power also suffer. Mounting evidence indicates that these children tend to experience peer rejection and lasting negative feelings about themselves, and there is danger that their mistaken behaviors may become more entrenched (Ladd & Price, 1987; Surgeon General's Report, 1999).

A teacher's decision to intervene in a conflict is neither easy nor pleasant, but sometimes plainly necessary. Teachers often watch to see if children can resolve a conflict on their own. They have no choice but to intervene, however, when a conflict is deteriorating, serious disruption is occurring, and/or the danger of harm is growing. Intervention that is firm and at the same time nonpunitive and friendly is the measure of a teacher's value of guidance in the encouraging classroom.

The two-part goal of conflict intervention is to coach the children to solve the immediate problem and teach the children skills so that they manage the conflict more peaceably next time.

The basic techniques teachers use to reach this two-part goal are

- guidance talks when an individual child is involved.
- mediation when a small number of children are involved.
- class meetings when the conflict affects most or all.

These techniques—all aimed at bringing productive communication to the situation—are discussed in Chapter 6. When a child is experiencing frequent and serious conflicts, the teacher uses *comprehensive guidance*, which includes the three basic resolution techniques above, *crisis management techniques* (discussed next), and the use of a comprehensive strategy worked out and applied cooperatively by staff, parents, and sometimes other professionals. A discussion of comprehensive guidance follows later in this chapter.

CRISIS MANAGEMENT TECHNIQUES

When conflicts cause emotions to intensify, crisis management techniques steer the teacher away from a common misimpression: that children "know better" and just need moralistic reminding in order to behave better. In fact, due to developmental immaturity, young children are just beginning the lifelong learning process of "knowing better." They may have rote knowledge of "right and wrong" and can tell you in a particular situation if they "were bad." But, young children have not yet mastered—as some adults never do—the management of their conflicting perceptions and feelings in ways that result in ethical decision making (Gartrell, 2003). During crises, children need friendly and clear teaching and not the punishment that comes with moral dictates (Katz, 1984).

Conflict management gives way to **crisis management** when a conflict—an expressed disagreement—is getting out of hand. Crises occur when emotions are running high, and the communication process is breaking down. (The conflict may not have completely deteriorated, but the teacher feels it is about to happen.) In crisis management, the teacher makes a final effort to restore communication so that mediation can take place. If civil communication proves impossible, the teacher works to restore order so that the basic conflict management techniques can be used when emotions have cooled. *In other words, the goal of crisis management is to restore the situation to where communication can occur, in order to solve the problem.*

Four crisis management techniques that are part of a guidance approach include:

- *being direct*
- *commanding a choice (including redirection)*
- *calming all involved (sometimes by separation)*
- *using physical restraint*

The techniques appear roughly in the order of use by a teacher as a conflict escalates into a crisis. Note that redirection and separation are included as options under broader headings, a reminder that these two techniques lapse into punishment when teachers use them as automatic responses. The crisis management techniques that follow assist teachers to manage their own emotions and to use guidance when emotions are running high.

1. Being Direct

Crises require direct teacher intervention. Yet confrontation as an intervention technique must be used with care. Especially when a teacher's emotions are rising, it is important to focus on the need to be firm *and friendly.*

Being direct is actually a collection of three responses that constitute *the crisis management method of first resort.* The teacher uses first resort responses when the situation is deteriorating, mediation for the moment looks doubtful, and the teacher wants to keep a crisis from becoming full blown.

Three ideas from Ginott (1972) provide a useful set of tools when harm or serious disruption is imminent and the teacher directly intervenes:

- describe without labeling
- express displeasure without insult
- correct by direction

Describe without Labeling

A first step in confronting a crisis is to describe to the children what you see. Describing events succinctly to the children lets them know why you are intervening—and helps the teacher pull thoughts together for what to do next.

With guidance, the teacher accepts the individual but not the individual's mistaken behavior. In a paraphrase of Ginott's words: Address the situation, do not attack personality (1972). The teacher describes what she or he sees that is unacceptable, but does so without labeling personalities, because "labeling is disabling."

> Example: *"I have heard loud words over here and seen hitting. This is not being friendly to our classmates. We need to fix this problem."*

Express Displeasure without Insult

Anger leads to mistaken behavior, in children and in adults. For this reason, even obedience-based discipline models maintain that teachers should not act out of anger. As Ginott points out (1972), anger is an emotion that all teachers feel; they either manage it or are controlled by it. Since they are in the business of guiding children to express emotions in acceptable ways, professional teachers need to model the management of anger themselves. The careful expression of displeasure, to show that you mean business but will not harm, is a necessary guidance skill. Ginott advocates the use of *I messages,* to report personal feelings without condemnation.

> Example: "You forgot our guideline about wrestling and Lionel got slammed. *I am really upset about this.* I want you to think of a way that you can help him feel better."

Correct by Direction

Correct by direction echoes a guidance basic: "Don't just tell children what not to do; tell them what to do." Direct children to alternative acceptable behaviors. Young children are still learning "what to do instead" and have a need for and a right to this guidance. If you won't tell them—sometimes more than once—you cannot expect them to know. The difference is between intervention that is punitive and intervention that can be educational.

> Example: "Voshon, I cannot let you hit anyone, and I will not let anyone hit you. *You need to take three deep breaths so we can talk about this. You need to use your words to tell him you are upset.*"

Using the Ideas Together

When teachers enter a situation, they inevitably add a new layer of complexity to the conflict. For this reason, the teacher uses the describe-express-direct sequence carefully. These techniques are guidance only when they restore boundaries and at the same time support self-esteem. Their purpose, like all crisis management techniques, is to restore civility so that problems can be talked through. Often in crisis situations, the "describe-direct" techniques, without the "express," are enough.

Example: "You are hitting. You need to stop and sit down. I will help you get calm so we can talk."

Expressing personal feelings, even when done professionally, tends to "up the ante." For this reason, the teacher does not make expressing feelings an automatic part of the intervention sequence, but consciously chooses when to express feelings. The teacher expresses displeasure only when she or he feels bothered by events and needs to get personal feelings "on the table." Sometimes the teacher decides that children need to know how their teacher feels—adults have feelings too. When conflicts have escalated to crises, the teacher often states personal feelings as a way of insisting that established classroom limits need to be respected.

Example: "You two are fighting and are angry and hurt. Fighting is not okay in this classroom. I am really bothered by this. You will sit down in different places. We will talk as soon as both of you and I have cooled down."

The purpose of being direct is to restore order so that problems can be solved, reconciliation achieved, and the safety of the classroom community reaffirmed. As with all crisis management techniques, the teacher describes, expresses, and directs in order to make conflicts manageable—not simply to bring a swift end to the crisis. The teacher who firmly intervenes—such as by redirecting a child to another area—but provides no follow-up, practices a form of what York calls "the power of silence" (1991). Failing to guide children to learn from a conflict means that children's feelings of hurt and anger may well continue unabated. The intervention has failed to rise above punishment.

Emotional outbursts warrant discussion—even if after a cool-down time. Even three-year-olds benefit from talking about it. True, what to say and how to say it (guidance talks) take practice. Listening carefully, responding with friendly respect, and trying to be brief help prevent the hands-on-ears reaction—a sign that to the child this is not a talk but a "lecture." The long-term effectiveness of guidance depends on talk, and words that are meant.

Example: "Are you feeling better now? (pause) That was quite a fracas (intentionally teaching a word). Tell me what you think happened. (long pause)."

2. Commanding a Choice

In a guidance approach the teacher matches the firmness of the intervention to the seriousness of the mistaken behavior. For example, at a prevention level, the teacher frequently *invites* choice making: "I need some super strong helpers to move these chairs." At a problem-solving level, the teacher *requests* choice making. "We have almost finished picking up. As soon as the books are on the shelves and the blocks are in the box, we can go outside."

At a looming crisis level, the teacher sometimes *commands* a choice: "Brett, you choose: Use words to tell us your feelings, or let's go to another part of the room to cool down and then we will talk." *Commanding a choice* is a form of correction by direction. Teachers use this technique when a quick intervention is needed and they feel they must "cut to the chase." Because of the emotional power in commanding a child to choose, it is *the crisis management method of second resort.*

When commanding a choice, the teacher is not forcing a "me against you" ultimatum—"Either you play nice or I will give you a 'red light'." Such ultimatums set up adversarial relationships between teachers and children and undermine mutual trust and respect (Greenberg, 1988). Instead the adult has children choose a personal course of action, teaching them that they have power in the situation. The child may not like the options, but the choice allows some dignity—in contrast to the "do it or else" alternative imposed by a threat.

In commanding choices there is an *in-choice* (the choice that the adult hopes the child will make) and an *out-choice* (the choice the adult prefers less, but still can live with). Typically, the in-choice is for the child to participate in a process that works the problem through. The out-choice is to cool down so the conflict can be resolved later. The teacher avoids out-choices that impose a predetermined "solution" for the child's mistaken behavior. In the midst of a crisis what seems a logical consequence to a teacher may really be punishment—so the teacher always gives thought to the "out" alternative.

For example, an out-choice for continued reckless play on a climber might be to go to a different activity and later discuss the situation; it would not be to stay off the climber for a week. A follow-up guidance talk that teaches safer behaviors is a key part of the procedure. Commanding a child to choose remains nonpunitive only if the out-choice is a logical consequence to the child and if guidance is later offered.

Some authors criticize the command of a choice, as by itself the technique does not help children realize the immediate and long-term benefits of mediation (Carlsson-Paige & Levin, 1992). When two children have a run-in and one or both parties elect the out-choice, the teacher often brings them together later, when feelings have cooled, and engages in mediation then. The follow-up is what keeps commanding choices in the "guidance camp." This guideline is why a teacher is more likely to command the choice, "We can talk about this now or you can choose to talk about it later when you are more calm," rather than "We can talk about this or you can sit by yourselves and think about how to use your words." The second out-choice is not one a young child can accomplish on his own and is really punishment (Katz, 1984).

Because of its power, commanding a child to choose is a crisis management method of second resort. But the technique does hold out the possibility of mediation to resolve the difficulty and so has its place for teachers when emotions are running high.

3. Calming Techniques

Teachers intervene in crises first by being direct, and second by commanding a choice. They use these techniques as first and second resorts when they perceive that children may still be calm enough to mediate the conflict. When children are too upset "to talk about it," the teacher tries calming techniques without formal separation, *the crisis management of third resort.*

Getting calm during conflicts is an ability all humans need. *Adults* have trouble talking through conflicts when their emotions are running high. Certainly young children, with months rather than years to build on, cannot. The teacher knows that conflict management must be delayed and crisis management used when children are too upset to talk. Children who are totally upset give the adult no choice but to help them calm down first and talk later. At the moment, feelings are all that is real for the child. Anything else, such as explaining the reasons for behaviors, will just add to the child's frustration. So, in using this method of third resort, the question becomes how to help the child calm down.

There are different terms for the most basic technique the adult uses: *reflective listening, active listening, acknowledgement of feelings.* Whichever term is preferred, the technique calls for the adult to give words to the emotions the child is showing, letting the child know that the adult cares.

Example: "Sharlene, the tears are flowing down your cheeks and you look so very sad. Would you like to sit on my lap?"

Example: "You hurt your foot when you kicked his shoe, and it hurt you again when he kicked you back. Let's just stay here for a few minutes until you feel better. Then we'll talk about how to solve this problem."

One other calming technique, when children have not totally lost control, is to have them take deep breaths, counting to three or five with them as they breathe. Counting to 10 without the breaths is another common technique. A teacher once relayed to me that she heard a three-year-old counting very seriously to himself: "1,2,8, eleventy, 10." She thanked him for counting to get control, and he said if he didn't he "would really get mad."

Separating to Cool Down

Sometimes the only way that teachers can help a child to calm down is by separating them from the situation. These "cooling-down times" are different from time-outs (Chapters 5 and 6). In the traditional time-out, a teacher isolates the child in a quiet place in the room *as a consequence* of being in the conflict. The teacher typically asks the child to "think about" what has happened. As mentioned, Katz (1984) points out that this request is developmentally inappropriate. Children can only begin to understand what happened if they are helped to do so by a guidance professional. Otherwise, they are likely to experience stress reactions, internalize angry and hurt feelings, and be reinforced in a negative self-labeling process.

When making the decision to remove a child from a group, the guidance professional asks and answers two difficult questions. *The first* is: Am I removing this child to cool down so we can talk later, or am I removing this child because of what he did (Gartrell, 2003)? The truth is that sometimes teachers separate a child as a way of expressing their own anger. Although there are worse things a teacher could do as a result of feeling angry, there are better responses to feeling anger than putting a child on a chair.

Instead of removal, if the child is not upset, a more fitting consequence may be to mediate the conflict. A child who has hurt another usually does not want to hear from the other child and the teacher about the hurt he has caused. But, within the framework of protected dialogue, this empathy building may be just what the child needs. The adult who can manage personal anger and actively work to resolve the conflict through mediation has mastered a high-level guidance skill.

The second question is: Will the child calm down more easily if I am near; or will my proximity reward the child and reinforce the mistaken behavior (Slaby, Roedell, Arezzo, & Hendrix, 1995)? The adult stays near a child to reassure against the punishing effect of removal, and to calm so that mediation can occur. Mediation for a child who has hurt another is hard work and not necessarily something to look forward to. A child who knows that forthright mediation is to follow "sitting out with the teacher," is not likely to find the teacher's presence reinforcing for the mistaken behavior.

Sometimes, however, teachers know a child well enough to recognize a need for personal space as part of the calming process. In this case, they get the child settled, give the child space to get calm, and facilitate the transition into mediation. Calming techniques, especially with separation, is the crisis management technique *of fourth resort.*

4. Physical Restraint

Some children experience violence in their lives (see Chapter 9), and as a result of strong emotional needs, act out against others. The payoff for aggression can be reinforcing for a child, and teachers must use firm but friendly words and actions to halt "an upward spiral of violence" (Slaby et al., 1995). The foundations of guidance are undermined if teachers allow children to hurt themselves or others. At the same time, the encouraging classroom promotes nonviolence in adults as well as children. The adult intervenes actively but neither punitively nor violently. "Grownups as well as children are *never* allowed to hurt anyone in the classroom" (Slaby, et al., 1995, p. 93).

The Crisis Prevention Institute (CPI, 1994) offers training "on how to use minimal-force restraint techniques that are appropriate, effective, and safe in given situations" (Slaby et al., 1995, p. 93). Especially with older children, CPI training is helping teachers learn to cope in violent situations. The following discussion of physical restraint, *the passive bear hug*, has been used by teachers of young children for many years.

Physical restraint is the crisis management technique of *last resort*. It is *not* any of the notorious methods of subtle or not so subtle corporal punishment used on children over time. Physical restraint is *not* paddling, spanking, slapping, ear pulling, hair yanking, back-of-the-neck squeezing, knuckle whacking, retribution child-biting, mouth taping, or binding to a chair. Neither is it pushing or pulling a child, nor hanging a child upside down.

Physical restraint means holding a child, including arms, legs, and perhaps even head, so that the child cannot harm you, other children, or himself or herself. Physical restraint is used when a child has lost control, physically and emotionally. A child in need of restraint may be attacking another child, the teachers, or another adult. The child may also show such behaviors as hitting body parts against a floor or wall.

Once the teacher decides that physical restraint is necessary, the commitment is total. Quickly removing the child's shoes is a helpful survival strategy. Sitting down and clamping arms around arms and legs around legs is what physical restraint is about. Children generally react strongly and negatively to being restrained. The teacher stays with it and often speaks soothingly to the child. With many children calm words or even quiet singing or rocking helps; other children calm down more easily with silence.

The passive bear hug provides behavioral limits that for the moment the child cannot provide for himself or herself. With the realization that the teacher is providing needed behavioral and emotional controls, the child calms down. Gradually, the child finds the closeness comforting and, strange as it might seem, the passive restraint sometimes ends as a hug. (Who needs the hug more at this point is an open question.) If the child becomes able to talk about the event at the time, the teacher provides guidance. Otherwise, guidance talk is provided at a later time. After physical restraint, children (and adults) are drained. Helping the child into a quiet activity, like reading a book, promotes reconciliation.

Whenever possible the teacher relies on the teaching team during crisis management, and certainly when passive restraint is used. One adult works with the group, keeping them as busy as possible. Another adult uses the procedure. In this day and age staff witnesses of the event are always

For the third time Dean had his block structure knocked down. This time the child was Latif, and Dean began shouting. Dean threw blocks at Latif and then hit and kicked at him. Neddie, the teacher, approached rapidly, saw that Latif was not really hurt, and said firmly "You're upset, Dean, but I can't let you hit or kick." When he began hitting out at her, Neddie took hold of his arms and legs, and sat down with Dean on the floor.

Dean shouted for Neddie to let him go, but she held on and began to say quietly, "Dean, I can't let you hurt anyone, and I won't let anyone hurt you. I am holding you so that no one will be hurt."

After struggling, Dean saw that the teacher would not let go and gradually became more quiet. Neddie told him that it was no fun to have things destroyed by others and that he had a right to be upset. She encouraged him to next time use words and to come to her right away. After a few minutes, she suggested that Dean do some puzzles, which he did. Dean later asked to sit by Neddie during snack—much to the teacher's relief.

Two adults in the room observed the encounter. They monitored the other children and gave Neddie their support. Later the three met with the director and filed a report.

important. For teachers who are alone with a group, this is one important reason for telephones in the classroom. A follow-up self-check by the teacher later in the day is needed: Did the teacher use a level of force necessary to prevent further harm and not cause more? Many programs have a written report system for when crisis intervention such as passive restraint is used. Class meetings to allay concerns in classmates who may have witnessed the events are essential—teachers work hard to restore a sense of safety in the classroom.

Coping with Our Own Feelings

A burden many early childhood teachers feel is that they are supposed to be angelically nurturing—when they really are just humans working very hard. Teachers too become upset, and teachers need to have calming techniques for themselves. Self-disclosure about feelings and counting to 10 are techniques teachers often use. On the other hand, a teacher told me this story about when she was having a bad day with her 23 kinder-gartners. She excused herself, went into the in-class bathroom, shut the door, and screamed. When she came out, 23 sets of eyes were staring at her. "Thank you, boys and girls," she said, "Your teacher needed a time out, and she feels much better now."

Teachers model the expression of emotions just as much as they teach them. It is important for teachers to anticipate situations and days when they may be more likely to get upset, make plans for these times, and follow the plans. Three methods teachers sometimes use are

- developing buddy systems with other adults.
- going to less stressful fall-back activities.
- intentionally "laying off" children and situations that may be flashpoints.

(Remember despite the stereotype, a teacher does not have to love every child, just figure out ways to fully accept each child as a worthy member of the group.)

If teachers experience recurrent feelings of anger or despair, these are signs of unmet needs in themselves. It is to teachers' lasting credit that they seek help for themselves when they need it. The courage to seek assistance, despite the obstacles, is the mark of the professionalism of the teacher (Gartrell, 2003).

The crisis management techniques discussed here support children so that when things get tough, self-esteem is not further deflated by teacher reaction. It is important to note that in the encouraging classroom. Guidance is taught throughout the day as a part of the curriculum, and not just when conflicts happen. The adult who models and teaches democratic life skills within the framework of an encouraging classroom makes guidance more effective when conflicts become crises.

COMPREHENSIVE GUIDANCE

There is no such thing as a bad kid, only kids with bad problems that need your help to resolve. The challenge is that these kids are often the hardest to like, even though they need a relationship with us the most (Gartrell, 2002, p. 41).

Any child can have a day when things start out wrong and go down-hill from there. If serious mistaken behavior continues for more than a day or so, however, management techniques in themselves are not enough. Repeated, serious conflicts in the classroom indicate a child is experiencing strong unmet needs for physical and/or psychological well-being. The child has run up against life problems that are bigger than the child. Though it may not seem so, the Level Three mistaken behavior by the child is a request for help.

Children who show Level Three mistaken behavior pose difficult challenges for the encouraging classroom. Gootman (1993), Heath (1994), and the Surgeon General's Report (1999) point out that a *comprehensive intervention strategy* with a child having strong unmet needs is likely to be more effective than traditional discipline responses (which tend to be based on punishment). Teachers may have to remind themselves more than once that the time and energy the child requires is an investment in the child's future. On the "up side" teachers do not need specialized licenses or advanced degrees to use comprehensive guidance successfully.

The strategy for comprehensive guidance we will examine here is an expanded version of the model introduced in Chapter 6 and mentioned in various other parts of the text. Of necessity, the strategy starts with intervention to prevent harm and disruption—using the crisis management techniques discussed earlier in this chapter. The strategy also calls for learning more about the child, providing consistent guidance interventions, collaborating with other adults in a coordinated response, improving the level of teacher-child relations, and enhancing opportunities for the child to experience success.

Comprehensive guidance strategy includes some or all of the seven steps that follow. In some situations not all of the steps are necessary—such as the conference and written plan. In other situations, when informal application may not be working, a structured procedure becomes necessary, including a conference and development of an **Individual Guidance Plan.** This seven-step model illustrates the complexity of using comprehensive guidance with young children and their families. There is no getting around it: serious mistaken behaviors require comprehensive strategies to assist the child to cope with deep unmet needs and to teach the child social-emotional skills. After the model, a case study illustrates the steps in use.

1. *Build relations with the child and family prior to crises.* From entry into the program, the *teaching team* (lead teacher with any other classroom staff) develop relationships both with the child and family. The knowledge gained helps the team understand the needs, interests, learning qualities, and response styles of the child. This information is invaluable if a child should show strong-needs mistaken behavior. There is no substitute for positive relations already formed in the event that comprehensive intervention becomes necessary.

2. *Use guidance intervention techniques.* In the event of strong-needs mistaken behavior, the team uses the crisis intervention techniques previously discussed: being direct, commanding choices, calming methods, physical restraint, as well as the conflict management techniques of mediation, guidance talks, and class meetings. One teacher, usually the primary caregiver, may take charge in crisis situations, providing consistent limits, interventions, and follow-ups for the child.

3. *Obtain additional information.* The team seeks to understand the child's behavior and the child more fully. Adults complete two-part anecdotal observations, with part one describing words and actions and part two containing the teacher's attempts to understand what has been observed. Incidents of mistaken behavior are charted against days of the week, times of the day, and the daily schedule. Actions for gaining more information include talks with the child, discussions with staff, sharing notes and talking with the family, and (with permission) the input of other professionals.

4. *Use additional information.* The teaching team and all other staff working with the child meet. A key ingredient in the practice of guidance teaching—in everyday transactions as well as crises—is the inclusion of all staff (including specialists) working together as a team. While one teacher takes the lead in interventions, all team members provide support in modifying the program, preventing crises when possible, and improving their relations with the child. Improving adult-child relations is critical in comprehensive guidance. Unless staff consciously work at improving relations, their expectations may make it difficult for the child to change. The teaching team incorporates the information gained in their responses to the child. Follow-up contact with the family often happens after the initial "staffing."

5. *Hold the Individual Guidance Plan meeting.* If the first four steps do not result in resolution of the problem, a meeting is held with parents, teaching team, and other relevant adults to develop an Individual Guidance Plan (IGP). The team uses the problem-solving process of conflict management to develop the Plan. In writing the IGP, the team uses forms that have the steps of the process outlined.[*]

6. *Implement the Guidance Plan.* The team works together to put the IGP—development with the family—into operation. Consistent, nonpunitive crisis intervention is a part of the plan. *One component of plans* is improvement of the relationships between the child and adults. Another is adaptation of the program to increase the child's opportunities for success. Referral for assessment by special education or other professionals may be part of the IGP. Counseling or other services may then be included. If special education services are warranted, an IEP may supersede the IGP.

---

[*]Readers can access Individual Guidance Planning forms on the Delmar Learning Web site at http://www.earlychilded.delmar.com
Click on the link for Online Resources™ where you will find the Online Resources™ to accompany *A Guidance Approach for the Encouraging Classroom,* Third Edition by Dan Gartrell. The IGP forms as well as other guidance materials are available at this site.

7. *Monitor Guidance Plan.* The staff continues observations, reviews the plan, communicates with parents, and makes modifications as needed. If necessary, the staff holds follow-up IGP meetings and acts upon modifications decided.

THE CASE OF GERI

In spring of 2002, I taught a class at Bemidji State University in northern Minnesota on the use of comprehensive guidance. Eighteen Head Start and child care teaching staff attended, including four family child care providers. The class met for two days in March to learn about the comprehensive guidance process. Over the next six weeks, each student completed an IGP with a child in their class, kept a record of what happened, and wrote a draft report. Over two days in late April, each student shared their drafts, received helpful feedback from small groups of class members and instructor-leaders, and prepared and submitted final reports.

"Geri's" story is influenced by the IGP studies of these students. I am presenting the case as an illustration of how comprehensive guidance works rather than a factual representation of a single case study. A summary of class findings from using the IGP procedure concludes the chapter. Geri's case follows the seven steps of comprehensive guidance.

1. Build Relations with the Child and Family Prior to Crises

Geri had been in the child care program since January and now in March had just turned five. Her mom was a single parent with two other children, an older brother and a younger sister. Since joining the program, Geri had always been very active and independent, seldom settling down in activities and acting quickly on impulses without apparent awareness of consequences. The teaching team (of a teacher, assistant teacher, and student teacher) enjoyed her enthusiasm and worked hard to help her manage her quick impulses while building a positive relationship. They noted that Geri liked dramatic play, could "hold her own with the boys," and enjoyed art and books. She had some difficulties settling in and staying with the group during circle times.

Geri's teacher, Veronica, met twice with the Mom, and found her a bit quiet and sometimes seeming close to her limit with managing the family. To keep in touch with Mom, Veronica talked with her at pick-up and drop-off and phoned her every two weeks to let her know how things were going.

2. Use Guidance Management Techniques

Over about a month, almost daily, Geri experienced conflict around following directions, showing defiance toward adults, and displaying domineering behavior toward her classmates. Gradually Geri began to show behaviors that the assistant teacher described as "sneaky aggressive." When she thought she wouldn't be caught, Geri shoved a child down, hit a child, or took something away. When confronted by a teacher, she would angrily deny that she did anything, or try to toss it off with a quick "I'm sorry, I won't do it again."

One day, Veronica saw Geri hitting a four-year-old in a corner by the fence on the playground. Macom had his arms up and was trying to push Geri away, but was not hitting back. Veronica got over there quickly and separated the children. She noted a clinched expression on Geri's face, and as Geri started to hit, her teacher held the child firmly: "This is hitting and there is no hitting at school. Both of us will sit down, now!" She sat down still holding Geri, both to comfort and restrain. Macom's assistant teacher arrived, having followed Veronica, and sat down with her arms around Macom. Veronica took the lead, "Please both of you take three deep breaths, Geri you too, one, two, three."

Before she could say anything more, Macom said loudly, "You are not s'posed to hit. You use your words. That hurt, and I don't like it. I am not your friend."

Geri had been struggling against Veronica's passive restraint. Her eyes were tightly closed and she was repeating, "You let me go!" When Macom spoke, Geri stopped and listened. Her expression went from angry to miserable and her body lost its rigidity and became limp. The teachers decided this was not a time for mediation. The assistant teacher tended to Macom and they went over to a bench and sat a while.

Veronica held Geri for a few minutes—long for this child—and using reflective listening told her, "You were very angry, so angry you had to hit, and now you look sad."

She gave Geri *wait time* and Geri said, "He bumped me and I hit him."

Veronica replied, "He bumped you and that made you upset. I wonder what else gets you angry, Geri?" Geri did not respond. After a few minutes, Veronica said, "Would you like to stay out here by me, or go inside where Sam (assistant teacher) is getting ready for lunch?"

Geri said inside, so they went in, and Veronica briefly mentioned to Sam that Geri could use a friend. Geri watched Sam for a while, then helped him finish setting the table. Geri ate little and slept a long time at rest. Afterwards she and Veronica had a guidance talk. They discussed what happened, how everyone felt, how Geri could make things better, and what she could do differently next time so that no one would be hurt. Veronica kept the tone friendly and the talk fairly brief. She afterwards helped Geri get started in a quiet activity.

3. Obtain Additional Information

Veronica wrote up the incident, and shared it at a meeting with the teaching team at the end of the day. That night she called Raylynn, Geri's Mom, but discussed the incident carefully, aware that Raylynn had a lot on her plate already. She asked Raylynn if there were any changes at home that would help in understanding why Geri seemed to be having some difficulties lately at school. Raylynn paused, then said that the father of the youngest child had moved in, and they all were having some trouble adjusting. Veronica noted this and told Raylynn if there were anything they could do at school to help, to let her know.

The team did not see other crises quite like on the playground, but Geri kept up her very active pace with the new wrinkle that she became frustrated very easily. The team was contending with daily bouts of very dramatic loss of emotional control. They also noticed that Geri was showing more aggression toward other children and the adults in the classroom. The team used specific, dated anecdotal observations to document the pattern they were seeing.

4. Use Additional Information

Veronica talked more with her teaching team early the next morning. They agreed Geri might be showing stress from the transition in her family. Veronica decided to use the play time before breakfast to spend 10 to 15 minutes of "just Geri time." The assistant teacher and student teacher greeted children and got them into activities while Veronica worked with Geri. Veronica explained to Geri that she needed to get to know Geri better and to be a good teacher for her. Each morning she gave Geri a choice of quiet activities to do, and the two moved into some space in the hall to be together. The other members of the teaching team as well found a few quality minutes to spend with Geri. Sam sat with Geri during circle time and helped her focus. Maylene, the student teacher, made a point of reading books with Geri each day. The team decided an IGP meeting was needed.

5. Hold the Individual Guidance Plan Meeting

Veronica set up an Individual Guidance Plan meeting with the Mother. Veronica asked if Raylynn would like to bring her partner, but Raylynn said no. The team arranged with the director to have their group covered, and all were waiting at 4:30 on the day. Raylynn showed up at 5:45 and said she couldn't talk because her son was home alone. The next morning Veronica suggested that Raylynn bring her son with her, and the three siblings could play while they met. They set up another meeting.

This time the meeting happened. The team (including the student teacher) started with the interests and achievements of Geri. Raylynn knew there was a problem on the agenda, but still appreciated hearing "some good stuff." The team matter-of-factly went over their observations of some of Geri's mistaken behaviors. Raylynn commented about Geri's pattern of impulsivity with quick apologies, which she and the team had talked about before. Raylynn said the pattern was getting worse, along with "tantrums over little things." Raylynn seemed guarded in what she said about the home life. But they all agreed, Raylynn too, that Geri needed more positive attention.

Raylynn said she might try an idea she had heard about in Head Start. Once each week she would have two of the children stay with Grandma, and do something special that she would decide with the third child. She said she would start with Geri. She also agreed to allow an early childhood special education teacher to do an observation, relative to Geri possibly receiving special education services. Veronica asked if the family would like a home visit, but Raylynn said probably not at this time. They agreed they would meet again in two weeks.

6. Implement the Guidance Plan

Geri was "an angel" during the entire special education observation. The observing teacher remarked that Geri had a high activity level, but not abnormally so. She agreed to come back if the team asked. Veronica continued with her "just Geri times." One of Geri's favorite activities became writing and drawing "books" of three to five blank pages stapled together. One of her books was of Raylynn and Roger (the boy friend) fighting and a child looking on. The book ended with Geri "reading," "And then he goed away." Veronica wondered about this, but decided to discuss the matter only if Raylynn brought it up. With the increased positive attention from the team, Geri became less agitated and aggressive, but continued "to be her 78 rpm self." The teaching team decided that with reduced amounts of aggression and frustration, they could easily live with Geri's energy level.

7. Monitor Guidance Plan

During the next two weeks, Geri had days that went smoothly and days that had conflicts. Overall, the team found that Geri was having an easier time at school. Perhaps as important, all three teaching team members realized that they were feeling more attached to Geri. The assistant teacher admitted, "That kid used to bug me to pieces, but I understand her more now." In the follow-up meeting, cut short because the youngest child wasn't feeling well, Raylynn said Geri was having fewer tantrums at home. She also said that Roger was out of the house, but was still hassling her. Veronica and Raylynn agreed to weekly phone calls. In the first call, Raylynn mentioned that she had gotten a restraining order against Roger and "it would be hard for a while."

The team continued to stay in touch with Raylynn and to make Geri a fully accepted member of the class. They recognized that helping Geri make friends and fit in would build the child's sense of self and trust in the world, important for her progress to continue.

FINDINGS OF THE CLASS MEMBERS

This section discusses the findings of the class of eighteen early childhood professionals who completed IGPs for individual children in their classrooms and family child care settings. From their written IGP reports and discussion about them, some trends emerged that were reflected in Geri's story.

First, all the students that taught with other staff reported that the adults came together as a team in using the comprehensive guidance procedure. One teacher who was concerned that her staff were "on different pages about discipline" was surprised at the spirit of cooperation engendered by the project. Moreover, several students forged productive new collaborative relations with staff of other programs: Head Start and child care; Head Start and early childhood special education; child care and early childhood family education (a Minnesota-wide public school program), family child care provider with another provider, and church-based preschool and kindergarten. Class members expressed surprise at the number of their children attending—or eligible for services from—additional early childhood programs. Class members saw the networking resulting from the guidance plans as a definite plus.

Second, two family child care providers who worked on their own became a "phone team," talking often about their "cases." The providers also found themselves talking with other family child care providers as well. Without the benefit of an "in-room" teaching team, support systems for family child care providers around guidance issues are important. (Matters of confidentiality need to be respected, of course, whatever the teaming arrangement.)

Third, a majority of students reported improved communication with the family. About half of these students reported that they had positive relations with the family already, and the project caused them to join together even more. The other half (sometimes with hesitation) basically built (from scratch) teacher-family relationships during the project.

Fourth, six teams (totaling twelve students) found families cooperative as long as the intervention strategy did not go beyond classroom staff. In these instances, family members balked at "getting involved" with an early childhood special education teacher or a psychologist. Building on the trust relationship they had previously created, three other students were able to involve other professionals, either to do observations or through referral visits. Three other students were not able to extend services beyond what the program directly provided.

Fifth, the class felt positively about the experience of implementing a comprehensive guidance plan. All eighteen students wrote they had improved their relationships with their selected children and understood more how to work with them. At the same time, however, no student felt their case study children completely turned their lives around—that their efforts at comprehensive guidance "went perfectly."

Yet, almost all students were able to document progress in the children in relation to democratic life skills. Despite the fact that no one found a "magic answer" for their children's problems, the fact that their children were able "to get along better" is significant. The research of Ladd and Price (1987) indicates that children not able to fit in and make friends during their early years are statistically vulnerable for later problems in school and life as teenagers. Helped by their teachers to function in the classroom setting, these children are improving their chances of finding positive meaning in their schooling and their adult lives.

End Note: *The chapter is adapted from Chapter 10,* Problem-Solving Mistaken Behavior, *and Chapter 11,* Guidance through Intervention, *in Gartrell, D. J. (2003).* A Guidance Approach for the Encouraging Classroom *(3rd ed.). Clifton Park, NY: Delmar Learning.*

REFERENCES

Carlsson-Paige, N., & Levin, D. (1992). Making peace in violent times: A constructivist approach to conflict resolution. *Young Children, 48*(1), 4–13.

CPI (Crisis Prevention Institute). 1994. *Managing the crisis moment* [catalog]. Brookfield, WI: National Crisis Prevention Institute.

Gartrell, D. J. (2002). Replacing Time-out. *Young Children, 57*(2), 36–43.

Gartrell, D. J. (2003). *A guidance approach for the encouraging classroom* (3rd ed.). Clifton Park, NY: Delmar Learning.

Ginott, H. (1972). *Teacher and child.* New York: Avon Books.

Gootman, M. (1993). Reaching and teaching abused children. *Childhood education, 70*(10), 15–19.

Greenberg, P. (1988). Avoiding "me against you" discipline. *Young Children, 43*(10), 24–25.

Heath, H. E. (1994). Dealing with difficult behaviors—Teachers plan with parents. *Young Children, 49*(5), 20–24.

Katz, L. (1984). The professional early childhood teacher. *Young Children, 39*(5), 3–10.

Ladd, G. W., & Price, J. M. (1987). Predicting children's social and emotional adjustment following the transition from preschool to kindergarten. *Child Development, 58,* 986–992.

Slaby, R. G., Roedell, W. C., Arezzo, D., & Hendrix, K. (1995). *Early violence prevention.* Washington, DC: NAEYC.

Surgeon General. (1999). *Surgeon General's report on violence.* Washington, DC: Department of Health and Human Services.

York, S. (1991). *Roots and wings.* St. Paul, MN: Redleaf Press.

Using the Booklet, *Developmentally Appropriate Guidance*, as a Training Tool

So you take a deep breath and say, "Okay, we understand these guidance ideas. We are using them as best we can, and learning more about children and guidance every day. But how do we explain guidance ideas to parents and other professionals? A lot of people out there didn't have teachers, parents, or colleagues who used guidance, and they see what we do as being permissive and not giving young children a foundation for "academics." How do we explain guidance to these people—new staff, parents, educators from other places—that we have to work with?"

Well, good question! (Gosh, hmm, well I am a professor, so I probably need to say something like this:) Maybe a booklet explaining "developmentally appropriate guidance" and a report on a workshop concerning how to use the booklet as a training tool would help. Now in its third edition, *Developmentally Appropriate Guidance of Young Children* is a position statement and training guide published by the Minnesota Association for the Education of Young Children. (See Appendix.) It is a handy little booklet that explains concisely six principles of guidance for use with young children.

I have done a few workshops now on how to use the Guidebook as a training tool. For this chapter I have included a discussion of the ideas from one such group about how to teach adults using the booklet. I found their ideas interesting and worthwhile. As you continue in your own professional development, I hope you will find the ideas in this chapter interesting and worthwhile as well—and maybe help you answer your very good question.

Developmentally Appropriate Guidance of Young Children (DAG) is a combined position statement and training document developed by the Minnesota Association for the Education of Young Children (MnAEYC). The third edition is copyrighted 2002, and the booklet (of which I was a principal author) has promise as a training tool for use with staff and parents. The booklet, printed in full in the Appendix, begins with the MnAEYC Position Statement on Guidance including a statement of six principles of developmentally appropriate guidance. The booklet then discusses each principle, including at least one example to make the principle's intent clear. The attractive and handy design of the booklet, as distinct from the straight-ahead narrative in the Appendix, makes purchase of the booklet worthwhile for many training purposes. MnAEYC can be contacted at http://www.aeyc-mn.org or by phone at 1-651-646-8689.

Chapter 11 discusses how to use the booklet as a training tool. The discussion builds from a college workshop organized by Western Community Action Head Start of Marshall, Minnesota, held on July 18 and 19, 2002. At the workshop numerous small groups analyzed each of the six principles for (1) the importance of the principle to the team; (2) issues parents and other professionals might raise about the principle; and (3) strategies for resolving the issues raised. Ideas from the two-day training serve as the basis of this discussion, which for each principle separately addresses *Importance, Issues,* and *Responding to the Issues.*

To provide a context for the reader, MnAEYC's Position Statement and summary of the six principles, which begin the booklet, follow:

A POSITION STATEMENT OF THE MINNESOTA ASSOCIATION FOR THE EDUCATION OF YOUNG CHILDREN

This position statement of the Minnesota Association for the Education of Young Children is the third edition of a document first published in 1989. Its intent remains the same: to give direction to the use of developmentally appropriate guidance with young children aged birth to eight.

The importance of guidance techniques that are based on sound child development principles has been well established, made even more so by events of violence in our schools and society since the initial edition. Now in the 21st Century, our ability to guide children's development in ways that result in what Piaget called "autonomy" (the ability to make decisions intelligently and ethically) has become a paramount education priority. By responding to classroom conflicts in ways that teach rather than punish and include all in the group, rather than exclude some from the group, teachers of young children are contributing to a more peaceful world.

This document is intended for use by administrators, teachers, and all other caregivers of young children. The term "teacher" is used in a general sense to refer to all adults who care for young children. **Guidance** is defined as an approach to children's development in which conflicts are viewed as teaching and learning opportunities; the adult helps children learn from their mistakes, rather than punishing them for the mistakes they make, assists children to learn to solve their problems, rather than punishing them for having problems they cannot solve.

Teachers who use guidance are sometimes firm but always friendly, protecting self-concept and respecting feelings so that children do not come to label themselves as behavioral failures. MnAEYC holds that teachers of young children should use guidance that is educational in tone and responsive to the child's level of development rather than using punitive discipline.

Principle One: The teacher uses guidance in order to teach children democratic life skills.

Principle Two: The teacher regards classroom conflicts as mistaken behavior and uses conflicts as teaching opportunities.

Principle Three: The teacher works to understand the reasons for children's behavior.

Principle Four: The teacher builds and maintains an encouraging classroom in which all children feel welcome as fully participating members.

Principle Five: The teacher uses developmentally appropriate practice to prevent institution-caused mistaken behavior.

Principle Six: The teacher functions as a professional rather than a technician.

PRINCIPLE ONE

The teacher uses guidance in order to teach children democratic life skills.

Importance of Principle

For the workshop groups studying Principle One, its importance lies in the fact that learning democratic life skills will carry through an individual's whole life. The skills of expressing strong emotions in nonhurting ways, working productively with others no matter the human differences, and making intelligent, ethical decisions are essential for general success in school and life. If young children make progress with these skills, they have a foundation that will make all future learning less challenging. Progress in these skills enhances self-worth and social competence, necessary for successful functioning as a member of a class and other social groups as the child grows, and group activities on the job during the individual's professional life.

Issues with the Principle

The groups concluded that many parents and some professionals "are not going to understand right away" the connection between how teachers guide children on a day-to-day basis and children's learning of democratic life skills. Some adults may misinterpret the understanding that teachers show about the connection as "permissive"—the "spare the rod and spoil the child" argument.

These adults haven't conceptualized that teachers need to have understanding about the mistakes children make in order for teach children to learn from them. They have not yet recognized that guidance techniques go beyond the immediate conflict situation to teach long-term skills for getting along.

They probably have not heard of the term *democratic life skills,* nor discussed that democratic life skills are difficult even for adults to consistently use. A related view is that children are too young to be able to learn democratic life skills. An assumption is that they should be learning basic academic skills instead.

Responding to the Issues

A first step in responding is to ensure that the staff have common training in the use and discussion of the principle (actually all six). If the entire staff has a common orientation, a support system will be in place for educating parents and other professionals. Where programs have developed cross-program partnerships, such as Head Start with child care providers—staff members of these programs also need orientation to the approach and should be included in initial training sessions.

Staff training suggestion: Have personnel in teams of three each discuss one of the democratic life skills (listed under Principle One). Using the opening that differences in view are to be respected, have each team discuss the implications of their principle for teacher-child, teacher-fellow staff, teacher-parent, and curriculum implications. The team works to understand differences in views among members and shares back with the groups the results of their discussion. The leader extends discussion of each principle to whole group. Goal: Staff will note they have many more points of agreement than disagreement about the principle. Staff will gain experience in discussing different viewpoints in ways supportive of all views. Guided discussion of this principle, and the others as well, will give staff practice in using the principles with parents and other professionals. Others will see that developmentally appropriate guidance is the unified approach of the staff.

PRINCIPLE TWO

The teacher regards classroom conflicts as mistaken behavior and uses conflicts as teaching opportunities.

Importance of Principle

In the words of one workshop team, "When we understand this concept, we have more realistic expectations of children and a better understanding of our role as an educator." The problem with the term *misbehavior* is that this term causes many adults to leap to judgment about the child, that is, "You are being naughty." Considering conflicts as mistaken behaviors—all children make mistakes in learning democratic life skills—Principle Two empowers adults to teach for social-emotional development, firmly if necessary, but always with total belief in the child and in the child's ability to learn. The *high expectation* of the teacher is that the child makes clear progress in learning democratic life skills—in order to succeed in school and life.

Issues with the Principle

Groups reported that some adults may object to what they see as permissive teaching in this view. These adults may think that the classroom will be too unstructured. For these folks, the classroom should provide preparation for the world of academics (school) rather than more abstractly teaching children how to solve problems. In terms of their own parenting, they may conclude, "My parents treated me this way and it worked. The child needs to learn that I won't tolerate naughty behavior done on purpose." Another possibility is that parents may not feel they have the time or the skills to use this approach in the home. They may give up on the approach too readily and separate themselves from the program's approach.

Responding to the Issues

An accepted first step in working with parents in early childhood programs is to build trust through productive teacher-parent relationships. Starting from the beginning, home visits, letters, phone calls, e-mails, greeting-meetings all should be for the purpose of building positive relations. At greeting-meetings, by way of introducing the program to parents, staff discuss their "reframing of discipline as guidance" in order to teach children self-discipline. Staff share simple written materials, or use the DAG booklet. They may also use videos to illustrate both mistaken behavior and how to teach when it occurs. Staff reiterate that the purpose of guidance is to begin teaching the lifelong democratic life skills. In the process of learning these skills young children, with only limited opportunities and experience, make mistakes—even if their actions seem deliberate. In follow-up meetings, staff work with small groups to better personalize content for parents and to enlist support from parents familiar with the program approach.

For professionals in other programs, staff prepare and present materials that represent the program's approach: "We could create a statement about what our program teaches and *why*. Share this with other professionals (kindergarten teachers, early childhood special education staff) instead of *them* just giving written expectations to us." Work in a unified and positive way to encourage a paradigm shift among collaborating professionals.

PRINCIPLE THREE

The teacher works to understand the reasons for children's behavior.

Importance of Principle

In the words of one small group, "It is important to understand the motivation for behavior so a teacher can decide how to respond." Children might hit or use unfriendly words because: "a life experiment" gets out of hand; they have been influenced to show the mistaken behavior by significant others (including action figures); or they have unmet physical or psychological needs and are acting out against the world. The teacher also wants to determine whether the conflict is caused by a dispute over property, territory, or privilege—the three most common sources of problems in early childhood classrooms (Dinwiddie, 1994).

A teacher who figures out the motivations and sources for the conflict has vital information for acting intelligently to help the child learn from the situation. The teacher uses observation skills, communication with the child or children involved, and communication with other members of the teaching team to understand as much as possible what happened and determine the nature of the guidance intervention.

Issues with the Principle

Adults sometimes find it easier to blame a child than to figure out what actually happened in a situation and show positive leadership. They may label a child's personality and "believe that behavior cannot change without punishment." In relation to one's own child, a parent may take the child's behavior personally, as a reflection on them. The parent may find it hard to understand that there is a reason for the behavior other than a "defect" in the child's character.

Responding to the Issues

An important understanding for the teacher to convey is that children are in a developmental process. Conflicts happen not because children are "bad," but because they are just learning the skills they need to solve social problems civilly. "In learning democratic life skills children, like all of us, make mistakes."

The teacher might invite the adult into the classroom. When there is a "break in the action," help the parent understand why a conflict has occurred, and why he or she responded in a particular way. The teacher might educate the adult about the importance of not labeling a child who has frequent conflicts. Instead explain that the child is at the beginning of a complicated learning process. Because of life circumstances, the learning may be going slowly, but the child is just starting and he or she is still learning. Understanding the child, rather than just blaming, makes it easier for the teacher to guide the learning that the child needs to do. Other members of the teaching team can reinforce these reasons for understanding children's behavior so that the adult knows this is the program's approach, rather than a single teacher's.

PRINCIPLE FOUR

The teacher builds and maintains an encouraging classroom in which all children feel welcome as fully participating members.

Importance of Principle

Teachers who build encouraging classrooms ensure that all children feel valued and avoid dynamics that make some children feel more valued than others. As one group mentioned, "It is important to make everyone feel welcome and valued with something to contribute. Because it doesn't feel good to be excluded in any way, shape or form."

By not singling children out either for praise or criticism, and instead showing acceptance of all the children in the class, the teacher prevents some children from feeling that they are not worthy and do not belong. Over time, "outcasts" often singled out for their behavior, develop lasting negative feelings about themselves and the institutions they find themselves in. In the teen years, these young people may identify with gangs or cults and act out on the basis of their feelings of rejection and resulting stress. Others may turn angry feelings inward and contend with mental health issues such as depression and addiction. Children who feel that they belong as worthy members of the class have less need to act out against themselves or the world.

Issues with the Principle

Adults who themselves experienced classrooms in which traditional discipline was practiced may not understand the encouraging classroom. The expectations of these adults about young children, their behavior, and their educational performance may not be developmentally appropriate. They may fail to see that teachers do enforce consequences for mistaken behavior, but the consequences have to do with the child learning more acceptable ways of expressing emotions, not with threatened or actual removal from the group. Adults—both parents and other professionals—may lack a support system, so making reinforcement for using guidance difficult to come by.

Responding to the Issues

As one group stated, "If we can approach a parent and have them realize how they felt themselves when they didn't feel safe or were left out—and how at school we want the children to feel safe and welcome—wouldn't they want the encouraging classroom for their kids?" In a meeting, have parents work in groups of three and recall episodes when a teacher used punishment (often embarrassment) with them or a classmate. Have the small group select one example and figure out a different response a teacher might make to teach a child a positive lesson from the experience. Have the small groups share and point out that teaching positive life lessons is what the encouraging classroom is about. Discuss the importance of an encouraging environment for the child both at home and school, but do so in a way that offers support for the parent who wants to try to use more guidance.

For other professionals, share the research by Ladd and Price (1987) and Ladd, Kochenderfer, and Colemen (1996) that children who are able to make friends and find a place in the group during early childhood are more likely to experience academic and social-emotional success right on through high school. Ladd and colleagues' research shows that children who cannot find an acceptable social place in early childhood classrooms have a much higher risk of dropping out and having serious behavioral difficulties. "Use Columbine or another school shooting as an example of what can happen when children don't feel safe and a part of the group."

Ask the adults to meet in small groups and recall an incident when a teacher helped a child who was vulnerable for exclusion from a class to fit in. Suggest they recall an incident that involved either themselves as a teacher or a child, a classmate, or a child of their own. Then discuss with the whole group how it feels to be excluded—or despite vulnerabilities included as a full member of the class.

If parents and other professionals have been able to visit and observe the encouraging classroom at work, use anecdotes from the classroom. Stress the importance of the teaching team working together to bring about an encouraging classroom. As one group commented, "It's like teaching an old dog new tricks. It might be better to model and show results first. Have them relate to their own experiences and have stories from your classroom at hand." With adults as well as children use your ability to be understanding rather than relying just on patience.

PRINCIPLE FIVE

The teacher uses developmentally appropriate practice to prevent institution-caused mistaken behavior.

Importance of Principle

The groups recognized that programming, which takes into account the development and experience of young children, reduces the mistaken behaviors that children do not cause so much as fall into. An example is limiting large groups to avoid restlessness. Teachers recognize that development, experience, and learning style differ in each child. Teachers continuously review, and if necessary modify, all parts of the program to improve responsiveness to each child. Such program components include:

- classroom designs
- daily schedules
- curriculum activities
- grouping arrangements
- cultural attitudes
- behavioral standards and intervention methods

The sentiment expressed in the group reports is that developmentally appropriate practice means that teachers give children the best possible program they can, given each child's development and experience. The role of the teacher is not to "prepare" children for the next level, when expectations for that preparation are not developmentally appropriate.

Issues with the Principle

Many adults, parents as well as other professionals, believe that preparation for the next level includes rote cognitive skills such as the ability to name colors, shapes, letters, numbers, and increasingly the sounds of vowels and consonants. Preparation in the social-emotional domain for these adults means compliance in such matters as respect for teachers and peers. The adults may not find these parts of the program being emphasized and not see these bits of knowledge emphasized in the assessments done by staff. They conclude that children are "playing too much and not learning anything."

Responding to the Issues

At the beginning of the year teachers may wish to put out an easy-to-read "Guidebook on the Education Program in Our Class" that addresses these concerns. Staff who come together to develop such a guidebook will be working out their own unique viewpoints on these issues. Reference to the *Guidebook* as the year goes on can be helpful as reminders to parents.

As a "modern" explanation about cognitive development, teachers can point out that brain development occurs fully when the child is engaged in an active ("hands-on"), satisfactory learning process. Through repeated successful opportunities to interact with materials and people, children develop their brains, and their thinking and speaking abilities in the process. We look for progress in cognitive, verbal, musical, artistic, and physical thinking, rather than the recitation of facts, as indication of educational achievement. (Memorization and recitation can be a small part of this process if there is not undue pressure on performance—the activities are kept playful—and as long as adults realize that children may have limited understanding about the symbols they can name.) As to social and emotional development, teachers refer to the democratic life skills and use observation and careful communication in assessing and reporting children's progress toward them.

There was concern in the groups about the emphasis by authorities outside of the program on measurable "academic achievement" rather than authentic educational progress. The concern is that persons who have power over programs do not understand how young children really learn.

PRINCIPLE SIX

The teacher functions as a professional rather than a technician.

Importance of Principle

For one group, this principle is about "teachers becoming better at working with children and recognizing their actions and how they affect children." For another group, the principle indicates the teacher's ability to "examine the situation; calm down and then model for the child how to handle democratic life skills with other children." A third group commented that the principle means a teacher "replaces discipline with an understanding of mistaken behavior and guidance."

Issues with the Principle

Parents may not understand the teacher's responses to mistaken behavior, helping children to solve their problems rather than punishing them for having problems. They "don't always agree that a child should express his viewpoints—they may feel the children are talking back." As well, parents may not know their importance in helping teachers to be professionals and use guidance.

Other professionals may not have had the same training or orientation, and not be aware of the difference between technicians and professionals. They may be wary of critiquing other co-workers and instead distance themselves from teachers trying to be professionals and use the guidance approach.

Responding to the Issues

Explain the philosophy at the beginning of the year, and ask "for parent volunteers to help with the process" of using guidance. Teachers model what being a professional is about and "Carefully explain to parents this is what we did and why." Encourage and support parents in their own process of personal development.

Frank discussion with other professionals can help them understand the concept of being a professional teacher. Encourage these adults to recall experiences when a teacher reacted in an "automatic" way without fully understanding a situation. Explain that the program encourages and supports the professional development of staff, and that begins with putting aside automatic reactions to "misbehavior" and movement toward professional judgment about how to help children learn from mistaken behavior. Emphasize that "Professionals learn even as they teach."

End Note: *This chapter was written specifically for this book. Additional information about the booklet* Developmentally Appropriate Guidance *is available from the* Minnesota Association for the Education of Young Children, *St. Paul, MN.*

REFERENCES

Dinwiddie, S. A. (1994). The saga of Sally, Sammy, and the red pen: Facilitating children's social problem solving. *Young Children, 49*(5), 13–19.

Ladd, G. W., Kochenderfer, B. J., & Colemen, C. (1996). Friendship quality as a predictor of young children's early school adjustment. *Child Development, 67,* 1103–1118.

Ladd, G. W., & Price, J. M. (1987). Predicting children's social and emotional adjustment following the transition from preschool to kindergarten. *Child Development, 61,* 99–103.

Other works used are those stated in the *Developmentally Appropriate Guidance* For Further Reading section, given in Appendix.

Developmentally Appropriate Guidance of Young Children (Third Edition)

A POSITION STATEMENT OF THE MINNESOTA ASSOCIATION FOR THE EDUCATION OF YOUNG CHILDREN

This position statement of the Minnesota Association for the Education of Young Children is the third edition of a document first published in 1989. Its intent remains the same: to give direction to the use of developmentally appropriate guidance with young children aged birth to eight.

The importance of guidance techniques that are based on sound child development principles has been well established, made even more so by events of violence in our schools and society since the initial edition. Now in the 21st Century, our ability to guide children's development in ways that result in what Piaget called "autonomy" (the ability to make decisions intelligently and ethically) has become a paramount education priority. By responding to classroom conflicts in ways that teach rather than punish and include all in the group, rather than exclude some from the group, teachers of young children are contributing to a more peaceful world.

This document is intended for use by administrators, teachers, and all other caregivers of young children. The term "teacher" is used in a general sense to refer to all adults who care for young children. **Guidance** is

175

defined as an approach to children's development in which conflicts are viewed as teaching and learning opportunities; the adult helps children learn from their mistakes, rather than punishing them for the mistakes they make, assists children to learn to solve their problems, rather than punishing them for having problems they cannot solve.

Teachers who use guidance are sometimes firm but always friendly, protecting self-concept and respecting feelings so that children do not come to label themselves as behavioral failures. MnAEYC holds that teachers of young children should use guidance that is educational in tone and responsive to the child's level of development rather than using punitive discipline.

SUMMARY OF PRINCIPLES FOR DEVELOPMENTALLY APPROPRIATE GUIDANCE

Principle One

The teacher uses guidance in order to teach children democratic life skills.

Principle Two

The teacher regards classroom conflicts as mistaken behavior and uses conflicts as teaching opportunities.

Principle Three

The teacher works to understand the reasons for children's behavior.

Principle Four

The teacher builds and maintains an encouraging classroom in which all children feel welcome as fully participating members.

Principle Five

The teacher uses developmentally appropriate practice to prevent institution-caused mistaken behavior.

Principle Six

The teacher functions as a professional rather than a technician.

Principle One

The teacher uses guidance in order to teach children democratic life skills.

A typical purpose of traditional classroom discipline has been to keep children "in line." When teachers make this purpose a priority, they tend to use discipline techniques that rely on "blame and shame" and slide into punishment. Embarrassment-based discipline—singling children out, scolding, using time-out—causes children to feel unwelcome in the group and unworthy. Children may begin to fall into a self-fulfilling prophecy and have more, not fewer, problems in the classroom.

The purpose of guidance is to teach children the **democratic life skills** they need to be healthy individuals and productive citizens. Democratic life skills include the ability to

- see one's self as a worthy individual and a capable member of the group.
- express strong emotions in non-hurting ways.
- solve problems ethically and intelligently.
- be understanding of the feelings and viewpoints of others.
- work cooperatively in groups, with acceptance of the human differences among members.

Democratic Life Skills Are the Outcomes of Guidance

The attainment of democratic life skills, more than scores on standardized tests and other measures of academic achievement, will keep our society strong, just, and free.

Example: Two children first argued then hit and kicked each other over sharing new miniature family figures. The teacher did not take the figures away from the children and give them a time out for fighting. The teacher did separate the children to cool them down and bring them together to resolve the conflict. After discussing the conflict, the children (with the teacher's help) decided that one child would have his two adult figures run "the store." The other child would bring in his rather large family and buy "lots of food and stuff." (This was not the solution the adult anticipated, but the children were satisfied so the adult went with it.) The children agreed that next time it would be better to use their words or get the teacher to help rather than fight.

Principle Two

The teacher regards classroom conflicts as mistaken behavior and uses conflicts as teaching opportunities.

Democratic life skills are a lifelong endeavor. Some adults never learn them and most of us have to work hard to use them consistently. Children, with only months of life experience and brain development (a five-year-old is only sixty months), are just beginning to learn these complex skills. In the process of learning, they make mistakes. For this reason, a teacher who uses guidance views the conflicts that children have not as misbehavior, but as **mistaken behavior.** This shift enables the adult to think about what she or he can teach children as a result of the conflict, not what she or he has to do to the children for having it. The shift in attitude empowers the adult to be a mediator and teacher rather than rule "enforcer."

Example: Damon didn't make it back from the playground in time and wet his pants. Charissa saw this and with Delray began calling Damon "piss pants Damon." While the class was coming in and finding things to work on, the teacher got Damon dry clothes. She then had a guidance talk with Charissa and Delray. She told them she once wet her pants at school and asked them if they had ever had an accident and wet their pants. Charissa said she did once. Delray said he didn't but his little brother did. The teacher got the children to say how Damon probably felt and then asked them to think of some ways they could help Damon feel better. Later in the day, the teacher smiled when she saw Charissa talking with Damon. She smiled again when she saw Damon and Delray playing together.

Principle Three

The teacher works to understand the reasons for children's behavior.

There are always reasons for children's behavior. Working to understand these reasons can assist the adult in helping the child. Although we can never know another person fully, we can increase our understanding and that effort in itself can lead to better relations and progress in learning democratic life skills.

Children do things to see what will happen. Children learn from such actions, and others' reactions. Sometimes "experimentation mistaken behavior," if harmless, should be ignored. If the adult decides to intervene, she or he should do so in a way that teaches the child about consequences and alternatives, but also appreciates the child's natural curiosity: the child's need to learn.

Example: A child marks on a table. "Maria, you can color on paper. Let's get some soapy water and wash the table. Then we'll get some paper to use with those markers."

Children do things because they have been influenced by others to do them, either at home or in the classroom. With "socially influenced" mistaken behavior, the adult firmly but matter-of-factly reinforces a limit, but also teaches an acceptable alternative for next time.

> *Example:*   Child says, "that damned kid makes me so mad." Teacher (hiding smile) responds: "Peter made you feel upset, and you can tell him or me, but you don't need to call names. We'll get the message."

Children show strong needs (serious) mistaken behavior because they have trouble in their lives that is beyond their ability to understand and manage. Sometimes the trouble can be physical, such as an undetected illness or injury. Other times, the trouble may be caused by a serious situation at home, center, or school. When a child shows rigid or extreme behavior, the adult should be alerted to the need for more information, especially if the behavior continues for more than a day or two. Observing and talking with the child can often add to an adult's understanding. Meeting with other staff can be helpful. A phone call or conference with parents may well be essential to better understanding the problem. Occasionally, consulting with an outside professional can help. When staff fully use their resources for understanding what is going on, a coordinated comprehensive guidance plan is easier to construct.

> *Example:*   A teacher notices that a child shows uncharacteristic irritability especially toward the beginning and end of each week. Talks with a parent determine that the parents have separated and the child is living with the mother during the week and the father on the weekends. The staff works together with the parent to make the transitions more understandable and less traumatic for the child.

Children with serious problems may show them in the classroom because it is the safest place in their lives. These children are asking for help, inappropriately perhaps, but in the only way they can. Often, they are the most difficult to like, but need a positive relationship with a teacher the most. With such children MnAEYC cautions against the use of such labels as "challenging" or "difficult"—even if the terms have intervention programs behind them.

Labels easily cause a teacher to become overly sensitized and to only notice the challenging or difficult behaviors. She or he may miss productive behaviors and admirable qualities in the child and give feedback that is distancing and negative. The child may feel stigmatized, disqualified from group membership, at a time when a sense of belonging is crucial for healthy development. The label a child receives may stick even with future teachers and in future classrooms. Whenever a young child is labeled as a result of having problems, rather than being helped to resolve them, schooling becomes more difficult.

Principle Four

The teacher builds and maintains an encouraging classroom in which all children feel welcome as fully participating members.

Informally defined, an encouraging classroom is a place where children want to be when they are sick as opposed to not wanting to be there when they are well. Trust and acceptance are the foundation of the relationship between an adult and a child. In the encouraging classroom, the teacher is able to build this foundation with every child, even those children who experience frequent conflicts. Except in rare circumstances, which always involve the family and often involve other professionals, the child's status as a member of an encouraging classroom is not up for debate.

In the encouraging classroom, the teacher does not need to love each child—teachers are human and not angelic—but as a professional, the teacher does need to build with each a working environment of trust and acceptance. The reason is that children who gain the understanding that they are valued and belong tend to develop positive self-concepts and have less need to act out against the world. With all children in the encouraging classroom, the teacher's goal is the same, to assist in making progress toward democratic life skills. All of the children are special, just because they are in the class. Some children just need more time and extra help to learn the skills, because life has given them a longer road to go.

Three practices mark the encouraging classroom. **First,** the teacher does not single out children for either praise or criticism. She or he acknowledges individuals privately; then they know the encouragement given is really meant for them. He or she addresses public acknowledgement to the group as a whole. In both cases, the teacher understands that acknowledgement is often more needed by learners as encouragement during the learning process than as praise given after the task is completed.

Example: The children in my class were making story pictures of thanks to send to the rescue workers in New York after the World Trade Center tragedy. I was really impressed with their efforts and said, "I like how you are all working so hard on your story pictures. Your work shows such thought about all the rescuers did." After I made this comment, I noticed several children smiling as they worked. Some even complimented their neighbors' pictures. One child had made a very detailed picture and was printing "Thk u fr hlg." She said, "But I don't think they could read it." I knelt down and put my arm around her shoulder. I told her I could read it, and did. She said "Yeah, maybe they could" and she wrote more words on her picture that I also read back to her.

A **second** practice of the encouraging classroom is that traditional discipline techniques like time-outs and names on the board are replaced by guidance methods like conflict management, guidance talks, class meetings, and comprehensive guidance. We saw an example of conflict management under principle one (the two children fighting over the figures), an example of a guidance talk under principle two (with the two children calling a third a name), and an example of comprehensive guidance under principle three (the child who was experiencing split custody with her parents).

Teachers hold class meetings, even with prekindergarten children, when conflicts in the class become public and affect many members. Instead of traditional punishment of the whole group, the teacher meets with the class to try to resolve the problem together. Guidelines for class meetings typically are that anyone can speak; we need to listen carefully to each other; we tell the truth; we appreciate and respect each other.

> *Example:*   An early childhood class had to walk down the hall of a school to reach the gymnasium. A few teachers complained to the principal that the children were being too loud as they walked down the hall. The teacher held a class meeting to solve the problem. After the children discussed the problem, the teacher asked if anyone had ideas about how they could remember to walk down the hall quietly. One child said, "I know, we can be mommy and daddy elephants who have to tiptoe so we don't wake the babies." To the teacher's amazement, the other children liked the idea. As they walked down the hall the next day, the principal loudly complimented the class. "Ssh," said one of the children, "You'll wake the babies!"

Third, the teacher works with other adults, both teaching team members and parents, to form partnerships that anchor the encouraging classroom. To children, anyone bigger than they are is a teacher. "Official" teachers in encouraging classrooms work hard right from the beginning of the year to build partnerships with other adults. With parents, the teacher might send notes home, make phone calls, do home visits, set up e-mail systems (with some), and generally take the lead to let parents know their involvement and input in the conduct of the class is important.

Orienting all staff (and regular volunteers) to guidance ideas through meetings, workshops, and booklets (like this one) are important. Staff together might make a handout of their own guidance ideas and use this as a basis of discussion with parents. Children who see significant adults in their lives modeling democratic life skills with each other will understand more fully that these skills are important to learn.

> *Example:*   A teaching team consisting of lead teacher, assistant teacher, teacher aide, foster grandparent, and special education teacher met to discuss upcoming parent conferences, to go on this year during the school day. The teacher asked for ideas about how this could happen. The staff agreed on a plan which had these parts. The already established parent corner in the classroom was, with the addition of more comfortable chairs, where the conferences would happen. Each conference would include the lead teacher and one other adult who

knew the child well. The other adults would implement a theme planned for the week, which included several independent center activities. The teaching team met with the children to explain what would be happening and that whatever adult was with them was to be their teacher. The children took an active interest in seeing that the plan worked, and the staff felt like a true team, as the conferences were held relatively hitch free.

Principle Five

The teacher uses developmentally appropriate practice to prevent institution-caused mistaken behavior.

Much mistaken behavior children do not cause as much as fall into. Institution-caused mistaken behavior is often the result of pressures teachers feel to "get children ready for the next level." While we all have a right to expect educational accountability—that children learn productively given their age, development, and experience—as professionals we need to work to reduce the effects of political accountability—the ill informed views of some politicians and administrators that children perform at token high profile levels come whatever. As a veteran kindergarten teacher once said, "My job is not to prepare children for first grade. It is to give them the best possible kindergarten experience they can have."

In the interest of educational accountability—and sometimes to curb the influence of political accountability—teachers monitor and change practices in their classrooms that unintentionally invite mistaken behavior:

- Group activities that require too much sitting and listening.
- Projects and lessons that have prescribed results too easy for some and too difficult for others.
- Schedules that fail to provide balanced routines and efficient transitions.
- Competitive expectations and evaluation techniques that make some children feel like "winners" and some like "losers."

Young children "are wired" for hands-on, active, personally relevant learning experiences that fully engage their minds and their bodies. When teachers recognize that children will be more able to perform the tasks of traditional classrooms when they are older—and won't necessarily benefit from "rehearsal"—they understand the connection of developmentally appropriate practice and guidance in the encouraging classroom.

Example: In a kindergarten class of 24 children the teacher had centers set up around the edges of the classroom for reading, "house," and blocks and trucks. The teacher felt pressured to have both a math focus and reading focus right away in the morning "while the children were fresh," and just let the children who were finished use the centers before recess. Gradually, he noted frustration among the children with this arrangement, as the slower workers were not getting time within the centers, some children were rushing their work to have center time, and the children in the centers had to quit soon after they started. Moreover, he noted that the centers seemed too crowded, and some children used the large open center area of the room as a raceway for the trucks. In fact, a couple of the boys referred to this area as "the track."

After attending a workshop on active learning, the teacher added a writing center, art center, music center, science center, and technology center. He spaced the centers around the room to eliminate runways, and clustered them by estimated activity levels. He scheduled an open center time between the academic focus times and asked the children to plan the centers they intended to use and record in journals (with early writing and art) what they did. His morning schedule became more productive, and he began to weave center use into his "focus" times and his periodic themes.

Principle Six

The teacher functions as a professional rather than a technician.

Teachers who are technicians react to conflicts in the traditional ways of their classrooms, frequently using discipline that slides into punishment. Rather than seek to understand the mistaken behavior and proactively teach alternatives to it, they react in a knee-jerk manner, enforcing rules to keep children obedient to the authority of the teaching staff. Teachers who are professionals attempt to replace stock reactions to mistaken behavior by using guidance to build an encouraging classroom and teach democratic life skills. As professionals, teachers make decisions about how to respond to behavior based on their judgments of the events at the time.

Still, because they are human, sometimes teachers may jump in too quickly, overreact, show inconsistency, lose their tempers, or otherwise show human frailties. Just as they encourage children to, teachers who are professionals attempt to learn from their mistakes. They know that their job is challenging because young children are just at the beginning of learning democratic life skills. They have accepted the fact that being a caring professional means modeling as well as teaching these skills every day, all the time.

When upset, teachers use methods to diffuse and express their feelings that do not put down the other person. They may pay attention to the "victim" first and talk with the child who did the hurting after they've cooled down. They may use "I messages" to describe their feelings rather than accuse and disparage the "culprits." They may firmly request more information before they make a hasty judgment. They may check themselves before responding to a child who is difficult for them to understand.

They may work with others who know a child or family better than they. They monitor their moods and feelings, aware of their impact on teaching effectiveness.

Examples: "Skip, I saw what happened. You need to wait here until I find out if Jenny is all right. We'll talk about it in a few minutes when I've calmed down."

"I am really bothered that the water got spilled out of the aquarium. We need to fill it up quickly and then we'll talk about what happened."

Finally, and most important, teachers recognize that they are learners even as they are teachers, and they continue to learn even as they teach.

Examples: ■ Teachers and caregivers participate in peer assessment including observation by and of other professionals in order to get feedback and engage in personal review of teaching practices.

■ Teachers use collaborations with parents, staff, and outside professionals in order to continue learning about the children they work with.

■ Teachers read, attend courses, conferences, and workshops in order to update their store of ideas.

■ Teachers use observation and communication skills to learn from the best of all teachers, the children themselves.

End Note: *The author acknowledges the Minnesota Association for the Education of Young Children for permission to use* Developmentally Appropriate Guidance, *(3rd ed.) in this book. All other uses of this information requires permission of MnAEYC.*

FOR FURTHER READING

Beane, A. L. (2000). *Bully free classroom.* Minneapolis, MN: Free Spirit Publishing.

Betz, C. (1994). Beyond time-out: Tips from a teacher. *Young Children, 49*(3), 10–14.

Da Ros, D. A., & Kovach, B. A. (1998). Assisting toddlers and caregivers during conflict resolutions: Interactions that promote socialization. *Childhood Education, 75*(1), 25–30.

Elkind, D. (1997, November). The death of child nature: Education in the postmodern world. *Phi Delta Kappan,* 241–245.

Froschl, M., & Sprung, B. (1999). On purpose: Addressing teasing and bullying in early childhood. *Young Children, 54*(2), 70–72.

Gartrell, D. J. (2000). *What the kids said today: Using classroom conversations to become a better teacher.* St. Paul, MN: Redleaf Press.

Gartrell, D. J. (2001). Beyond time-out part one: Using guidance to build an encouraging classroom. *Young Children, 56*(1), 8–16.

Gartrell, D. J. (2002). Beyond time-out part two: Using guidance to maintain an encouraging classroom. *Young Children, 56*(2), 36–43.

Harris, T. T., & Fuqua, J. D. (2000). What goes around comes around: Building a community of learners through circle times. *Young Children, 55*(1), 44–47.

Lawhon, T. (1997). Encouraging friendships among children. *Childhood Education, 73*(4), 228–231.

Logan, T. (1998). Creating a kindergarten community. *Young Children, 53*(2), 22–26.

McClurg, L. G. (1998). Building an ethical community in the classroom: Community meeting. *Young Children, 53*(2), 30–35.

Schreiber, M. E. (1999). Time-outs for toddlers: Is our goal punishment or education. *Young Children, 54*(4), 22–25.

Weber, N. (1987). Patience or understanding? *Young Children, 42*(3), 52–54.

Approved by the MNAEYC BOARD—NOVEMBER, 2001, October 2002

DEVELOPMENTALLY APPROPRIATE GUIDANCE COMMITTEE

Dan Gartrell, Author	*Vicki Iverson*
Diane McLinn, Chair	*Ginny Petty*
Roz Anderson	*Zoe Ann Wignall*
Mary Holub	*Katie Williams*

Revised by Dan Gartrell and Nancy Johnson—September, 2001; June 2002

MNAEYC

1821 University Ave.

Suite 296-S

St. Paul, MN 55104

dfitzwater-dewey@aeyc-mn.org

INDEX